Algeria

Challenges and Chances in Global Higher Education

Leonie Schoelen

UNIVERSITY
JOHANNESBURG

UJ Press

Algeria: Challenges and Chances in Global Higher Education

Published by UJ Press
University of Johannesburg
Library
Auckland Park Kingsway Campus
PO Box 524
Auckland Park
2006
https://ujpress.uj.ac.za/

First published 2024

https://doi.org/10.36615/9781776489947
978-1-7764899-3-0 (Paperback)
978-1-7764899-4-7 (PDF)
978-1-7764899-5-4 (EPUB)
978-1-7764899-6-1 (XML)

This publication had been submitted to a rigorous double-blind peer-review process prior to publication and all recommendations by the reviewers were considered and implemented before publication.

Language Editor: Luke Perkins
Cover design: Hester Roets, UJ Graphic Design Studio
Typeset in 9.5/13pt Merriweather Light

Contents

In memoriam

Professor Uwe Schmidt
Irmgard and Eugen Schoelen
Christine, Hans and Rolf Groß-Luttermann

Acknowledgements

I would like to profoundly thank, and express my utmost appreciation to my family, friends and colleagues for their support and encouragement, in particular: Professor Marie Salaün, Dr. Abbes Sebihi, Professor Tahar Sahraoui, Professor Kamel Chachoua, Professor Latifa Negadi, Dr. Baghdad Benstaali, Professor Isabel Steinhardt and the mentee group, Dr. Akiiki Babyesiza, Professor Patricio Langa, Professor Emnet Tadesse Woldegiorgis, Dr. Nicole Meier, Professor Philipp Pohlenz, as well as my parents Eleonore Hettler-Groß-Luttermann and Georg Schoelen, and my sister Isabel Schoelen, with their partners, and my nephew Lando Paul Grabowski. I am further grateful to all my interviewees, institutional administrations, editors and proofreaders and the original research funder, Cusanuswerk e.V., Germany.

Dedication

To the Algerian people, the most hospitable I have ever come to know.

1. Rationale: Relevance and Ambiguity of Academic Freedom

Societies undergoing transformation in the Arab world have had to deal with social demand for access to education, as is reflected in, for example, universities' civil role (Al Amin, 2016), community service (Arifi, 2016), or the reproduction of social elites in academia (Sabour, 1988, 2001).[1] As can be observed in the Arab higher education space, there is a dilemma of 'publish globally and perish locally' and vice-versa (Hanafi, 2011) – meaning that those scholars who are visible internationally through their publications are not recognised or successful academically at home – as well as a topical 'crisis of research and global recognition' in Arab universities (Almansour, 2016).

On the occasion of the 50th anniversary of Algerian independence in 2012, the Algerian Ministry of Higher Education and Scientific Research (*MESRS*) published a review of higher education in Algeria. The then Minister in office, Rachid Haraoubia, stated:

> The premier mission of the university is that of forging awareness, enhancing abilities till their highest-performing level and promote what is trustworthy and just. Universities constitute the real fabric of democracy, to which we add, social progress and economic development.[2]

---

1   The former article entitled Homo Academicus Arabicus refers to Pierre Bourdieu's famous work Homo Academicus (1984).

2   (French original) La mission première de l'université est celle de forger les consciences, améliorer les aptitudes jusqu'à leur plus haut niveau de performance et faire valoir ce qui est fiable et juste. Les universités constituent le vrai levain de la démocratie, nous rajouterons, du progrès social et du développement économique.

(Ministère de l'Enseignement Supérieur et de la Recherche
    Scientifique [MESRS], 2013, p. 25).
The limited amount of research as an essential university
function, as well as an activity, can be observed in this
discourse, which reflects Algeria's position within an African
as well as an Arab setting. In this context, a recent heated
debate about the restitution of Algerian-born Nobel prize
winners – Albert Camus, Literature, in 1957, and Claude
Cohen-Tannoudji, Physics, in 1997, who were raised in
Algeria and whose work mostly originated in the country –
exemplifies what is at stake in the Algerian higher education
system. The former Higher Education Minister, Tahar Hadjar,
stated that Nobel prizes would add nothing to Algerian
university education, and that world-renowned Algerian
scientists should not have any special status in the country
(Ghanmy, 2018). Upon announcement at a press conference,
this message sparked a public outcry among Algeria's
academics. As illustrated herein, the Algerian university is
situated at a crossroads in terms of reorientation (Miliani &
Sebaa, 2021).

Since the first reform of the colonially inherited system
in 1971 (MESRS, 1971), Algeria has been endeavouring to
nationalise its higher education system. As pointed out by
Algerian diaspora scholar Aïssa Kadri in the early nineties,
historical analysis cannot be disconnected from any
transformation of the higher education system (Kadri, 1991).
This fact was reiterated by Algerian researcher Mohamed
Ghalamallah in the 2000s: 'The present situation of the
Algerian university is a product of its past'[3] (Ghalamallah,
2006, p. 31). Accordingly, the questions central to the study
outlined below reflect a strong linkage with the historical
dimension, and, indirectly, the influence and impact or lack
of the *legs colonial*[4] (Bayard & Bertrand, 2006), while explicitly
taking the present into account rather than only the past,

---

3   (French original) La situation actuelle de l'université
     algérienne est le produit de son passé.
4   Colonial legacy

in describing the status quo and determining the functions through their evolution.

However, the adoption and subsequent implementation of the Bologna Process from 2003 – commonly referred to as *Licence-Master-Doctorat (LMD)* reform in French-speaking contexts, points towards a change in policy towards internationalisation. At the same time, there is an increasing awareness about the absence of the voices of the so-called global South, indicative of a recent national intellectual initiative to stand one's ground and, though lagging in global visibility, claim one's place internationally (Guerid, 2012b, pp. 5–19).

This dual orientation, leading to conflicting and contradictory directives, is the starting point of an analysis of the role of the contemporary Algerian university, and its implications for the central actors in its system – namely, Algerian academics. A macro analysis has not taken place yet. From the 1970s to the present, numerous concepts have been reflected in policies that refer to the identity of the Algerian university; concepts that may co-exist, or that may have been prioritised by the government, as highlighted in the following.

1.1 Object of Study and Analytical Framework

Existing literature on Algeria tends to be outdated and treats higher education issues from an economic or purely managerial perspective, rather than from the basis of education sciences or sociology. The formulation of the study questions below derives from the conclusions drawn from the literature, yet they have evolved in an exploratory manner through data analysis. They aim to help counteract the lack of empirical – especially, qualitative – information about the past, present, and new and future roles of the university.

The overarching question this study addresses is: *Which implications do the degree of the Algerian higher education system nationalisation and internationalisation orientation have on institutional development as well as individual practices?*, and, specifically, the subquestions;

- What functions does the present-day Algerian university[5] incorporate, including in international comparison?
- How do Algerian academics cope with higher education system implications individually?
- What are Algerian academics' motivations?

Firstly, there is an expression of a transformation element in Algerian higher education, triggered by, and correlating with, increasing globalisation and thus pressures for system integration. Hence, the system is placed between the poles of the local versus the global in its orientation of system and the national versus the international, which is reflected in higher education policy. Secondly, the focus is on the comparatively new function of research as an emerging field, playing a key role in internationalisation adaptation processes. The undergoing transformation is made visible by its politically-prescribed priority. Thirdly, the lens is focused on those carrying out research: individuals within Algerian academia, in that their academic practices are an expression of individual adaptation strategies.

The operationalisation of the questions central to the study requires a concept of positioning, which can be found in a definition of university functions over the time of higher education institutions' global development from medieval to contemporary times, as a frame of reference independent of national or political contexts. Therefore, Manuel Castells' sociological theory of the four traditional university functions (Castells, 1993), which have been reviewed in an African context since the early 2000s (Castells, 2001), has been identified as one of the frameworks of analysis. It is complemented by Lüscher's ambivalences (Lüscher, 2011a, 2011b) and Bourdieu's forms of capital (Bourdieu, 1986) as adequate frameworks from the data analysis, which accounts

5   Although numerous types of higher education institutions do exist in Algeria, this study focuses on the comprehensive university status institution only, as the scholarly literature has been focusing on this type, and as the full university is the only form within the national higher education system featuring both teaching and research in its vocation.

4

for the individual academic's micro perspective, as opposed to the macro or systems level.

Based on this rationale, the object of study refers to individuals conducting or engaging in research in a particular national higher education system. In this way, the present missing link between the macro and micro levels will be identified and established. They are complementary in that they draw on each other: Castells addresses the macro level, Bourdieu addresses the expression on the micro level as a reaction to the macro level, and Luescher links the two by the ambivalences perceived on, and by, a micro level, which originate on the macro level. In addition, Castells' continuum of university functions evolving over time (Schoelen, 2023) may be posited against Bourdieu's forms of capital in that different forms are required to succeed in phases of prioritisation of university functions. The notion that cultural capital is decisive when research is on the individuals' agenda has been examined in an African context (Langa, 2010; 2011), confirming its usability and potential for exploration in this thesis.

Consequently, none of the approaches individually may explain the observed phenomenon, but in combination, they serve as a framework for analysis and explanation. Moreover, as will be shown, ambivalences are not limited to the individual level, as is depicted by Lüscher. Indeed, they may determine the macro, or systems, level as a whole, which is relevant and pertinent in an African context. In line with the modern era creating ambivalences, and demanding tolerance of these (Bauman, 2013), modernity in African societies is not an abnormality, as it is intrinsically ambivalent, and it is what it is due to historical contingency (Macamo, 2005). From this background, the postcolonial situation characteristic of many transforming societies plays a role, too. In the case of Algeria, the latter is of particular importance as the multilingual context is both a lived diversity yet also cause for, and a source of, conflict (Sebihi & Schoelen, 2020).

Due to the empirical nature of this work, with an applied element in the form of policy implications and recommendations, and given its tripartite composition, the emphasis is on the framework in its – particularly innovative – combination of constituents rather than an exhaustive account of each of the three components, which is beyond the specific scope.[6] It is nevertheless acknowledged that the concepts have been subject to criticism since Bourdieu's lifetime, and nearing two decades after his death. Furthermore, all three theorists are of European origin, which poses an epistemological issue: there may be a link to an inherent bias, an associated worldview, and a level of normativity.[7] Therefore, the concepts are not universally applicable as they are presented here, and need to be tested and questioned every time in their claim of portraying, and making sense of, reality in a given context; in this case, the Algerian higher education system.

1.2   Methodology

Document analysis as the first step is a qualitative social research method conducted to assess meaning as well as different dimensions of a topic, and an important part of triangulation of the combination of methodologies to study a given phenomenon in providing a broad overview (Bowen, 2009). It is a common first step of qualitative studies, setting and complementing the material basis in preparation for the ensuing empirical element. Public records in the form of policy documents (O'Leary, 2017) – while bearing in mind their official and sole-legitimacy nature, reflected in their voice and content – proved most useful in tracing the development and state of affairs of Algerian higher education as outlined in the following two chapters.

---

6   For this reason, exclusively primary sources are cited, and a more theoretically-oriented discussion is omitted in the following section.
7   These characteristics are also applicable to the author being of German nationality.

Expert interviews are characterised by their 'in-depth' nature and design (Yeo et al., 2014). Semi-directive, i.e., guideline-assisted expert interviews, were first conceptualised in the early 1990s (Meuser & Nagel, 2002).[8] They may serve

> (...) to shorten time-consuming data gathering processes, particularly if the experts are seen as 'crystallization points' for practical insider knowledge and are interviewed as surrogates for a wider circle of players. Expert interviews also lend themselves to those kinds of situations in which it might prove difficult or impossible to gain access to a particular social field (...). (Bogner et al., 2016).

Persons are interviewed because of their specialist knowledge of a context or phenomenon of interest in a social setting (Gläser & Laudel, 2010). In this sense, interview partners are informants rather than respondents (Gläser & Laudel, 2016).

Taking into account the type of centralised and bureaucratised higher education governance in the Algerian context,[9] the following dominant actor description characterises the setting, and guides the methodological approaches:

> The discourse on internationalisation is often dominated by a small group of stakeholders: higher education leaders, governments and international bodies. Other stakeholders, such as employers, and in particular the faculty and the student voice are heard far less often, with the result that the discourse is insufficiently influenced by those who should benefit from its implementation, (...) Internationalisation is evaluated too often in quantitative terms through numbers, or input and output, instead of a qualitative, outcomes approach based on the impact of internationalisation initiatives; (...). (Wit, 2016, p. 16)

---

8   For a detailed description of their situatedness compared to different types of interviews, see Lamnek and Krell (2016).
9   See chapter 3.1.

The methodological design of this empirical study addresses these issues by conducting qualitative interviews with Algerian academics, who are directly affected by implementation. By means of a qualitative study, the required systematic approach is adopted, based on '(...) feedback mode (...) of testing and recycling successive adjustments' which consists of '(...) goals, a data base, and predictive procedure' (Daghbouche, 2008, p. 76).

Accordingly, the study contributes to an empirical base that has been integrated into a recent project to tackle implementation challenges, after the Bologna Process of reform, by a needs analysis that employed qualitative methods and subsequent training of new lecturers in the processes of comprehension, action and evaluation (Benleulmi & Hadiby-Ghoul, 2015, p. 11). Recent studies (e.g., Ridwan, 2015; Bouab, 2016 [French Abstract]) and the focus on Algerian professors in recent dissertations[10] underline the key role that professors play in both the Algerian higher education system and its individual institutions, which justifies their selection as interviewees. In the Algerian context, the expert interview format is useful as it offers access to a non-political sphere and discourse, which would otherwise be extremely difficult, if not impossible, to obtain.

A total of 31 semi-directive expert interviews with one or two persons – from the same discipline, well acquainted with one other both from a professional context and personally – including professors of all disciplines, deans, vice-rectors, and numerous graduate students (master's/PhD level), were subsequently conducted at several different institutions in various urban or semi-urban settings in two main geographical

---

10   Bourenane, F. (2009). Syndicat autonome des enseignants du supérieur algériens. Entre action localisée et préoccupations nationales. Paris: Université de Paris VIII Saint-Denis. Fayçal, I. (2014). La contestation sociale en milieu universitaire en Algérie. Paris : Université de Paris VIII Saint-Denis. Toufik, M. M. (2013). Les enseignants universitaires algériens entre autonomie et instrumentalisation. Paris: Université de Paris VIII Saint-Denis.

regions of the country. These were conducted mostly in the form of focus group discussions. With the anonymity of participants, and thus also data protection, being the highest priority, some potentially identifying data including type or level of administrative and executive function had to be removed, as well as disciplines aggregated. For this reason, it was decided to refrain from including biographical data and other identity markers such as place, so that no correlation may be made.

Employing locally installed qualitative content analysis (QDA) software *f4*[11] (Dresing & Pehl, 2015), a first open thematic coding in category systems of first-order hierarchical structure (Saldaña, 2016) was conducted to identify relevant material following full transcription of the interviews. Qualitative content analysis (Schreier, 2013; 2014; Mayring, 2015) was chosen as a means of analysis, preceded by systematic coding following prescribed steps. Accordingly, the category system is a mix of deductive, i.e., theory-based main categories, and inductive, data-derived sub-categories. The main categories are composed of the four functions of the university (Castells, 1993; 2001) and Bourdieu's types of capital (Bourdieu, 1986), complemented by sub-categories created from the data. The aspect being coded is topic/theme and relevant material is included, observing the saturation criteria. The material is then segmented into units according to content criteria before developing a dynamic coding frame, which is amended in the process of data perusal. Coding is done in a hierarchical structure (first order). The results of the analysis are presented in a combination of typology and category system descriptions.

As for researcher positionality, the author is external to the context studied, but is familiar with the historical and cultural elements from having lived and worked in Algeria over three years. Furthermore, through collaboration and initiatives as well as activities, there has been extensive trust-building with university actors in positions comparable to the

---

11   https://www.audiotranskription.de/english

interviewees, as well as familiarity with their setting. From the author's experience, an outsider perspective – in this case, a German – is conducive to pursuing research in the form of qualitative data collection. The author has previously been perceived as neutral and pragmatic by the target group overall, which has facilitated her access and ensured cooperation and interest, as opposed to contrasting and rather biased or negative connotations associated with France-affiliated researchers. At the same time, she has observed attempts at influencing opinions in the course of data collection.

1.3   Academic Freedom and Institutional Autonomy

The rationale for the *Dar Es Salaam Declaration on Intellectual Freedom*[12] and the *Kampala Declaration on Intellectual Freedom and Social Responsibility*[13] in 1990 is outlined below.

The notion of academic freedom dates back to the Humboldtian educational ideal of the unity of teaching and research in Germany. It is connected to the concept of the modern research university. It traditionally encompasses three components: 1) freedom of inquiry and research; 2) freedom of teaching; and 3) freedom of expression and publication (Atkinson, 2004). First articulated on the other side of the Atlantic by Brown (1900) and taken up by the American Association of University Professors – the majority of whom were European-educated – in 1915, it was reviewed in 1925 and reiterated by the *1940 Statement of Principles on Academic Freedom and Tenure*.[14] In Europe, academic freedom was further conceptually developed based on the experience of Karl Jaspers in Nazi Germany (Iqbal, 1972) and his contemporary Michael Polanyi in Britain (Baker, 1978), the latter having co-founded the 'Society for Freedom in Science' in 1940.[15] Polanyi later famously described a 'Republic of Science' as a 'free

---

12   http://hrlibrary.umn.edu/africa/DARDOK.htm See part III on 'Autonomy of Institutions of Higher Education'.
13   https://digitallibrary.un.org/record/520822
14   See https://www.aaup.org/file/1940%20Statement.pdf (with interpretative comments as of 1970).
15   See McGucken (1978).

society' model (Polanyi et al., 2000) and the scholarly debate was subsequently resumed in an international scope (Birley, 1972). This expanded understanding was then first extended to India and African countries as Commonwealth members after independence (Ashby, 1966a, 1966b).

This concept, which is traditionally argued in a consequentialist way (Andreescu, 2009), applies to the micro (individual) as well as the macro system, in the form of higher education institutions.[16] As the right of faculty to teach and research freely, it is guaranteed in the constitution or by specific laws in most European and North American – as in the 1st amendment in the much-discussed case of the United States – countries, as well as in several Asian, Latin American, and African countries. For the European Union states, following a comparative analysis towards the end of the last decade (Karran, 2007), a 'Magna Carta' has been put forward in an attempt towards a unifying definition, given the legal challenges in the United States (Karran, 2009). Accordingly, in 2019, at the Council of Europe headquarters in Strasbourg, the 'Global Forum of Academic Freedom, Institutional Autonomy and Democracy' participants adopted and issued a Declaration.[17] Since 2000, a globally-operating organisation safeguarding academic freedom, *Scholars at Risk*,[18] providing temporary so-called 'safe havens' abroad and promoting the comparatively recently developed 'Academic Freedom Index',[19] has adopted the following definition:

---

16   While now dated, as of 2009, for countries in Europe, North America, and Australia, there exists an extensive open access research bibliography created by Terence Karran: http://eprints.lincoln.ac.uk/id/eprint/1763/2/ AcademicFreedomResearchBibliography.pdf. See also Kuhn and Aby (2000) for a US context-focussed, edited collection on an academic freedom literature review in the beginning of the millennium.

17   https://rm.coe.int/global-forum-declaration-global-forum-final-21-06-19-003-/16809523e5

18   https://www.scholarsatrisk.org/

19   See report as of March 2020, https://www.gppi.net/media/ KinzelbachEtAl_2020_Free_Universities.pdf, and working paper, https://bit.ly/4edLZJb

At-risk scholars at risk include professors, researchers, doctoral students, institutional leaders and other members of higher education communities who are threatened and/or attacked as a result of the content of their work, their status as academics or as a result of their peaceful exercise of the right to freedom of expression or freedom of association. (Scholars at Risk [SAR], 2020).

As is shown by the case of Algeria, higher education systems cannot be analysed in isolation from their socio-political, cultural, religious and linguistic contexts (Khelfaoui, 2012). While not only applicable in African contexts, violations or threats to their academic freedom have since prompted several social sciences researchers from the African continent to opt for exile or emigration. Among many others, examples of well-known African scholars in the field of higher education include Ali Mazrui and Mahmood Mamdani from Uganda, and Ngũgĩ wa Thiong'o and Paul Zeleza from Kenya (Zavale & Langa, 2018). Based on their personal experiences, they have since become advocates for the protection of academic freedom.[20] Perhaps less well known have been the Algerians Aïssa Kadri and Ahmed Ghouati, the late Houcine Khelfaoui, and anthropologist Fanny Colonna.

In addition to offering and safeguarding the affiliated individual's freedom, higher education institutions are competent to take and execute academic decisions, such as staff appointment and tenure, which functions have evolved as a principle as well as default right in the post-war decades in the United States (Leslie, 1986). In a dedicated 'Bill of Rights', three basic freedoms are to be granted to institutions, namely, non-government interference in institutional mission and strategy, budget autonomy, and definition of organisational structure and administration (Shirley, 1984). In principle, applying to public higher education institutions since the early 1990s (Ambrose, 1990), protecting the individual from any

---

20   Among others, see Zeleza (1997) and Mazrui (1975).
      See also Ndiaye (1996) for a West/francophone African
      assessment.

institutional paradigms – state or other, such as faith-based organisations – has been argued, again in a United States-originating debate, drawing on liberal democracy on the one hand, and corporate pluralism on the other (Gutmann, 1983). Likewise, traditional rationales refer to secular principles, which, however, have limitations in their actual application as they are primarily aimed at, for example, serving a particular group's interests, or spreading intra- or supra-societal values (Kirk, 1977; 1955). The effect of a particular dominating culture on academic freedom has also been exposed in states with a conservative orientation within the United States (Williams, 2006). Influence of this kind, among others, has led to a growing legal debate in the United States on the issue (Alexander, 2006).

Comparative studies on university autonomy have mainly been conducted in continental Europe and Anglo-American countries, or between the regions (Anderson & Johnson, 1998; Estermann et al., 2011; McDaniel, 1996). Asian and African countries have been included as objects of analysis to a lesser extent, and only comparatively recently. Related studies have been commissioned and funded by international bodies, with autonomy being discussed in the framework of higher education system reforms (UNESCO & Varghese, 2013; 2016). Corresponding to the observation that academic freedom is neither clearly defined, nor agreed upon, and not widely institutionalised (Altbach, 2001), institutional autonomy is much less common worldwide, with many universities featuring limited self-governance while structurally depending on the guidance of the respective political entity, in most cases, the national Ministry of (Higher) Education/Research. Indeed, the commonly employed North American setting is 'atypical' (Heisler, 2007). Instead, there is another perspective on academic freedom, which can be subsumed as 'between local powers and international donors' (Khelfaoui & Ogachi, 2011), but it must be highlighted that the latter is not universally applicable.

1.4   Algerian Higher Education Ambiguity

In the context of individual academic freedom and institutional autonomy, the notion of politicisation, in the sense of attributing a political meaning or dimension to higher education, or of the university, seems at odds. Hence, it is ambiguous and its meaning varies, depending on the context in which it is discussed. The politicisation of higher education, from an organisational point of view – especially in the context of incorporating higher education institutional autonomy – can mean that individuals, in the fulfilment of their function in representing an institution, are speaking on public policy beyond the academic or scientific sphere in the strict sense (Bloland, 1969). However, the opposite may very well apply, i.e., state intervention in academic affairs by institutional control, or employing scholarly discourse for political means (Wilson, 1997).

As described in the analysis entitled 'Higher Education and Differentiation on Knowledge: Algeria's Aborted Dream' (Khelfaoui, 2012),[21] power is exerted by those holding political influence, while having repercussions on the country's higher education system and its operation. In an environment where the state has long monopolised not only the provision of higher education but also taken decisions on scientific matters (Khelfaoui, 1996), and where political legitimation and social control have since superseded academic functions (Khelfaoui, 2003), there consequently exists an ambiguous relationship between actors outside of the formal political sphere, such as academics, and politics.

In the Algerian academic field, it can have a range of meanings: First of all, it may refer to the fact that politicians

---

21   This book chapter was previously published as a journal article in French; see Khelfaoui (2010). It was first presented during a CODESRIA conference, Academic Freedom and the Social Responsibility of Academics and Researchers in Africa: What are the new challenges?, Oran, Algeria, 9–11 March 2010. See https://www.codesria.org/spip.php?article674&lang=en for the agenda including proceedings.

or state authority-affiliated representatives take decisions unilaterally. Secondly, it may refer to the fact that choices are not of an academic but of an ideological nature. Thirdly, it may point towards directives coming from actors close to political power circles in the sense of the ruling party. Like the notion of *le pouvoir*/'power', in the recent so-called *hirak* movement of Algerian societal protest against the government, which may refer to the state in general, but also a particular group of people taking control after independence, le pouvoir is both an abstract entity and an actual group of people at the same time. This observation is reiterated by the previously referenced national higher education system macro analysis, with the conclusion that the political is superior to the academic (Khelfaoui, 2012), in the sense of:

> (…) the political sociology within which one can account for the effects of geopolitics and globalisation on the articulation of academic frameworks within academe (…) academic freedom, and the ability of academics to 'speak truth to power' are situated within the web of cultural, political, and institutional practices that enact them (Mazawi & Sultana, 2012, p. 28).

As a consequence, there is a conflict between professionalisation autonomy and institutionalisation control, which, in the case of Algeria, characterises the existence of, and the extent of the relationship between the scientific and political worlds (Khelfaoui, 2004).

2. Historical and Political Context

In this section, the historical and political context provides an overview of the People's Democratic Republic of Algeria. Drawing on the introduction, it sets the scene by first outlining Algeria's higher education history and policies as well as its higher education system development in particular in the subsequent chapter. The country's contextualisation starts with a profile and socio-historical overview before focusing on historical developments relevant to higher education.

2.1 The People's Democratic Republic of Algeria: Socio-Historical Overview

For centuries, the People's Democratic Republic of Algeria (Arabic الجزائر: *Al-Djazair*, 'rocky islands') has been strategically positioned, with more than 1,000 km of coastline on the Mediterranean Sea, which separates Europe and Africa. This geopolitical location has also brought about – contrary to many other countries formerly colonised by France – a unique status as an integral administrative part of France during its occupation for more than a century, starting in 1830. Today, more than half a century after independence in 1962, the emerging People's Democratic Republic of Algeria, the largest country of the African continent by area, is an essential actor in the Maghreb region and a member of the influential Arab league. In terms of urban and scientific infrastructure – for instance, with over 70,000 km of roads and almost 4,000 km of railway tracks, as well as hospitals, schools, universities, training centres, research laboratories and journals – Algeria ranks among the foremost countries in Africa and the Arab world.

Algeria's population of more than 43.5 million as of 2020 is predominantly young, with the majority under 30 years of age and almost 30% under 15. Its political system can be classified as a presidential republic. National holidays are celebrated on the 1st of November, the day of the revolution, and the 5th of July, day of the proclamation of independence. Algeria's official languages are modern standard Arabic – with the spoken Algerian dialect *Daridja* – and Tamaziɣt/Tamazight (so-called 'Berber'), which was awarded national language status in 2002 and became enshrined in the constitution in 2016. French continues to be widely used in administration, (higher) education and commerce. English is not currently widespread. However, the academic integration of the South, where neither French, nor the Northern-dominating Kabyl, a variety of Tamazight, is widespread, has led to a push for more English in the country's higher education system, as have representatives of science disciplines (Bensouiah, 2020b). In 2018, there were some 300,000 graduates against a backdrop of an illiteracy rate of 18.6% and an estimated 15% unemployment rate,[1] although the informal labour sector plays a role not to be underestimated.

Overall, Algeria's Human Development Index (HDI) classifies it as 'high human development', and ranks the country in the lower first half, at position 82 out of 189 countries. While above average for the Arab states, the HDI is slightly lower for females than for males due to differences of income and women's significant under-participation in the labour market, at 15% versus 67% (United Nations Development Programme [UNDP], 2019). Notably, Algeria is not a member of the World Trade Organization (WTO). Its ease of doing business index is in the lowest quarter of 190 nations and its global competitiveness index is in the last third of 141 countries (Germany Trade and Invest [GTAI], 2020).[2] 95% of its state revenues are based on exports from state companies' fossil fuel exploitation in the vast Sahara, which is indicative of a trade orientation towards Europe rather than the neighbouring Maghreb or sub-Saharan African countries. Nevertheless, alternative industries and services,

---

1   There are no specific statistics available on graduates' unemployment rate. See the empirical chapter for evidence related to the issue of the lack of data.

2   The figures mentioned in the remainder of this paragraph are taken from the same source.

such as construction, transport, logistics, communication and technology, are under development and increase by approximately 5% each year. Half of the imports are made up of foodstuffs, machinery, and chemical products, coming mainly from China and four European countries, but both exports and imports are in decline. Public and private investment makes up close to 50% of the GDP, 0,5% of which is spent on research and development, whereas debt accounts for almost half of expenditure. Foreign investment is characterised by a joint venture approach of 51% mandatory Algerian ownership. Likewise, foreigners cannot own land without a local counterpart.

A brief historical overview – which necessarily remains fragmented, though milestones in education and science are mentioned – has been included to account for Algeria's millennia-old history, to comprehend its importance as a melting point of cultures, societies, knowledge and languages between the East and the West, which is still true today. Algeria occupies a prominent place in the panorama of world prehistory. The number and the quality of its ancient relics, from the oldest palaeolithic to protohistory, give it an exceptional position and make it one of the first cradles of humanity. The first traces of human occupation, which marked Algeria's Prehistorical area, begin 2 million years ago and end with the first Libyan texts, called Tifinagh, in the 1st millennium.[3] The so-called Tighennif Man is the oldest known fossil human in North Africa.[4] The Algerian 'indigenous'[5]

3   See Sahnouni, M. The Site of Ain Hanech Revisited: New Investigations at this Lower Pleistocene Site in Northern Algeria, Journal of Archaeological Science, 1998, vol. 25, pp. 1083–1101, and Balout, L., Biberson, P. and Tixier, J. (1970) L'Acheuléen de Ternifine (Algérie), gisement de l'Atlanthrope, in: Actes du VIIe Congrès International des Sciences Préhistoriques et Protohistoriques, Prague, UISPP, 21–27 août 1966, pp. 254–261.

4   See Dutour, O., Le Peuplement moderne d'Afrique septentrionale et ses relations avec celui du Proche-Orient [archive], Paléorient, 1995, vol. 21, n° 21-2, pp. 97–109.

5   The author disapproves of this terminology, which is marked by quotation marks, due to its colonial connotation,

population, dating from sometime in the myriad before time, has been incorrectly referred to as 'Berbers', but this term derives from the Roman label 'Barbarian', and is of later origin. Another group, the 'Moors', refers to the later Arab Muslim presence, which continues to the present day. In fact, what is routinely portrayed as one people were many different civilisations – Moors (Mauri), Mauretanians, Africans, and many tribes and tribal federations such as the Leuathae or Musulami, none of whom share a common ancestry, culture, or language (Rouighi, 2019a). The modern, acceptable term for members of peoples in a multitude of countries is *Imazighen* (plural)/*Amazigh* (singular) (Rouighi, 2019b).

Ancient North Africa is divided into three groups, with shifting boundaries: to the West, Mauretania, which includes present-day Morocco and western Algerian; in the Centre, Numidia in the North, and the country of the Gétules in the South, while beyond the mountains, there are other nomadic 'Berber' peoples; in the East, the Punic space, where the Carthaginians dominate. The history of ancient Algeria is linked to that of the Mediterranean. The Libyan 'Berber' populations, whether nomadic or sedentary, participated in the economic and cultural movements of the region. Before the arrival of the Romans, Numidians ('Berbers') and Punics (Carthaginians) mingled in what corresponds to eastern Algeria.

Algeria, in antiquity, is marked by the emergence of kingdoms, during the Iron Age, over a period of approximately 1,500 years. The Phoenicians, in their efforts to extend their commercial network throughout the Mediterranean coast, established direct relations with the populations in northern Algeria from 1,250 BCE until the flight of Princess Elyssa (called Dido by the Romans) from the eastern Maghreb (present-day Tunisia), who founded Carthage there in 814 BCE.[6] The son of Juba I, named Juba II, was taken to Rome, where he received

---

yet – lacking alternatives – its use is adopted.

6   There is evidence that the Gétules, direct descendants of the branch of the Caspian civilization, having emigrated to the Sahara around 3000 before time, are probably those

a very advanced education, which allowed him to master several languages perfectly. He later married Cleopatra Selênê, daughter of Cleopatra VII of Egypt and Mark Anthony, general and friend of Julius Caesar. Holy Augustine, Bishop of Hippo Regius (today Annaba; 354–430 CE), the most prominent philosopher and theologist of early Christianity, who lay some of the conceptual foundations of Western thought and culture, was born and educated, and wrote, preached and died, in what is today Algeria. After his lifetime, a people called the Vandals, of Scandinavian origin, having been driven out of Europe, settled in Algeria for approximately one century (430-533) before their conquest by the East Roman Emperor Justinian I, thus making North Africa a Byzantine province.

The Arabisation of present-day Algeria took place through two (of a total of seven) large flows of populations arriving from the Arabian peninsula during the period of Islamisation. The first stage directly followed the Islamic conquest of the 7th and 8th centuries. This Arabisation was only superficial since it concerned only the conquered cities, where the Arabs settled, and constituted a scientific and aristocratic class that provided access to language, power and science to the rest of the inhabitants of these cities (Remaoun, 2000). The countryside remained purely 'Berber'. The dialects dating from this time are called pre-Hilialian (Meynier, 2007).

The second stage was the result of Bedouin incursions into Algeria in the 11th and 12th centuries, principally involving the Banu Hilal and the Banu Maqtil. This Arabisation was much stronger and deeper than the first, since it affected not only the cities but also the high plateaus, the plains and certain oases, leading to the gradual Arabisation of the country between the 15th and 18th centuries (Russell & Russell, 1999). The 'Berber' languages were maintained in the 19th century in the densely populated mountainous areas, the adjacent plains, and in certain oases of the South called 'Ksours'. The

---

who had the first relationships with the Carthaginians; the Prince of the Gétules proposed to marry Élyssa.

dialects resulting from this Arabisation are referred to as post-Hilialian (Hamet, 1932; E.B., 2001).

However, it should be noted that the influx of people from the Middle East has never been large enough to Arabise a majority of Algerians; assimilation rather took place through acceptance of the Arabic language by the local population on religious grounds. Linguistic Arabisation was therefore done mainly through the *Zaouïas* and religious brotherhoods, who used Arabic as the liturgical language and language of instruction, as well as by the political powers of the different medieval kingdoms of the Maghreb – who, with some exceptions, all used Arabic as the sole official language.

Consequently, in the mid-14th century, a university, in the modern understanding, with disciplinary departments, academic staff, visiting researchers, student residences, and scholarships, was established in Tlemcen (cf. Wadad Kadi),[7] in western Algeria, by a scholar, Abū l-'Abbās Aḥmad ibn Yaḥyā ibn Muḥammad ibn ʿAbd al-Wāḥid ibn Alī al-Wansharīsī, as the first institutionalised form of higher education[8]. Algerian ground-breaking intellectual, and commonly-regarded founder of modern sociology (Soyer & Gilbert, 2012), Ibn Khaldoun (1333-1406), who published a history of the Maghreb detailing successive Arab and 'Berber' dynasties as well as their Eastern and Western contemporaries, called 'The Book of Examples' (in Arabic), had taught there. It was similar in its academic programmes to medieval European universities of the time.

In the following century, in 1501, the Portuguese first launched an expedition to try to land on the Andalusian beach. After the occupation of the port of Mers-el-Kebir (1505), and that of the city of Oran (1509), the city was deserted, and

---

7   This university concept was then perfected and
     implemented in Fes, modern Morocco.
8   Barely disseminated, novel finding based on an unpublished
     script of an (undated) lecture available to the author,
     entitled 'The Madrasa in the Maghreb from the Sixth/
     Twelfth until the Ninth/Fifteenth Century' given by Wadad
     Kadi, Professor emeritus at the University of Chicago.

then completely occupied by Spanish troops. Their presence was short-lived overall and marked by rivalry with the Turks then installed in Algiers. Despite a Moroccan alliance against the Turks, the Spanish were then definitively expelled in 1555 by the Ottomans led by Salah Raïs Pasha. In 1575, Miguel de Cervantes, considered Spain's national poet to this day, while sailing, was attacked by Turkish ships, taken to Algiers, and subsequently declared a slave. However, as a bearer of letters of recommendation, Cervantes was considered by his captors to be someone from whom they could obtain a high ransom. He was, to use the expression of the time, a 'redemption slave' (Garcés, 2005).[9]

Ottoman Algeria, from 1516 to 1830, was associated with a period of a distinct, tradition-oriented Sufi culture and a maritime rule orientation, which sought to prevent North Africa's conquest by European Christians, as opposed to the Muslim Spanish Andalusian conquest. Rulers, who called the states of the region the 'Maghrib' as the Muslim West for the first time, overwhelmingly lacked knowledge of the Arabic language, and, hence, there was little recognition of the importance of learning, intellectual development and progressivist science beyond religious curricula. Coupled with political instability and bad governance, this lack of recognition led to the failure of educational institutions in the late 18th and early 19th centuries and widespread isolation. This state of affairs was reinforced by the Napoleonic conquests in Egypt, arousing widespread hatred against Europeans. There was also a second wave of Jewish immigration from modern Spain; these immigrants, having originated from Algeria, and

---

9   There is a theory according to which Cervantes would have started to write his most famous novel, Don Quixote, in Algiers. See Miguel de Cervantes (Author), Barbara Fuchs (translator), 'The Baghios of Algiers' and 'The Great Sultana': Two Plays of Captivity (2012), University of Pennsylvania Press; and Ahmed Abi Ayad, Alger : source littéraire et lieu d´écriture de M. De Cervantès, Insaniyat / انسانيات [online], 47-48 | 2010, first published online 08 August 2012, http://journals.openedition.org/insaniyat/4956.

escaped inquisition, reversed direction to return to Algeria. The Enlightenment movement of the time, on the other side of the Mediterranean, did not reach Algeria, and, therefore, the educational reform needed did not take place. Before French colonisation, the Arabic-language illiteracy rate was as low as 14% (Ladjal & Bensaid, 2014).

The French arrived in Algeria in 1830, to start what would be a 132-year occupation, until independence after a bloody eight-year liberation war, 1954–1962. After a brutal war and the defeat of leader Emir Abdelkader in 1847 and the annexation of the Kaybl region 1855, all subsequent uprisings by the local population were quelled until full control of the north of the country was established by 1881. Three regions, or *départements*, were then declared French territory. Algeria had had a special status in the French colonial Empire, which lasted from 1534 with the conquest of territory as *Nouvelle-France* in modern Canada, to 1980, with the independence of Vanuatu: Algeria was a *Département outre-mer* (after the second world war, *DOM-TOM*), and, therefore, an integral part of France, as opposed to other occupied countries in North or West Africa, such as Morocco or Senegal, which were protectorates. The impacts of French colonialism systematically destroyed Algerian identity through prohibition or eradication of cultural, religious and social structures. The population at the time was divided by discriminatory land ownership, language and religious policies (Merrouche, 2007) in a 'divide and rule' approach, inciting long-lasting animosities between Arabs, 'Berbers', and Jews. As French subjects, they had no citizens' rights, so 'Algeria became a part of the French national saga branded with phantasms of racialist ethnicism' (Meynier, 2014, p. 13).

Educational failure was such that, by 1901, there was a higher than 90% illiteracy rate due to suppression and confiscation of endowments that allowed the operation of schools, thereby closing existing Islamic institutions (Ladjal & Bensaid, 2014). A segregationist school set-up, combined with an aggressive *francophonie* policy, and the colonial administration's primary interest in exploiting the country's vast natural resources, led to total neglect, to the extent that, as late as during the first world war, the proportion of school-age Muslim children in primary school was less than 10% of an age cohort (Kadri, 2007), and, at the time of independence, 90% of the population was still illiterate.[10]

While Algerians fought for the French during the second world war, there was no sign of granting independence afterwards. The 1st of November 1954 marks the beginning of the Algerian Revolution in a bloody eight-year war of independence. 1,5 million people were killed both in Algeria and in France, making up a quarter of the population at this time. To this day, France has not formally apologised for the atrocities committed. In the months before and following independence, sealed by signing the *Evian accords* in March 1962, one million French and Europeans (the so-called *pieds noirs*) as well as 100,000 so-called *harkis*, Algerians who supported the French government and army, left Algeria overnight due to fear of retaliation, including lynching, even though they were legally protected.

As a brief summary, independent Algeria's foreign policy can be characterised as 'National Liberation Promoter to Leader on the Global War on Terrorism' (Zoubir, 2015), as it adopted these roles within the framework of the Organisation for African Unity (OAU), the African Union (AU)'s predecessor. Advocating African nations' increased influence in global politics as an advantage for the developing world in decolonisation and fighting neo-colonial Western interventionism, the People's Democratic Republic of Algeria represented, and aligned with, so-called 'revolutionary' states in the 1960s and 1970s. By the end of the decade, it already had 11 embassies in sub-Saharan countries (Mortimer, 1970). An example is the support of Zimbabwe's cause – formerly called Rhodesia – to quell British rule, by repeated high-level delegations at the United Nations (UN), and boycotting the General Assembly in protest over apartheid.

---

10   See Kadri (2007) for a comprehensive history and detailed statistics of school-level education in colonial Algeria.

Although little known in the West, during then-President Ahmed Ben Bella's international orientation, Algeria hosted several important continental conferences, including the Pan-African cultural festival in 1969, with Cuban and Brazilian revolutionaries also in attendance, and hosted military training camps, such as for the Mozambican independence party led by Eduardo Mondlane, and even as a residence of later governments as in the case of Angola. Algeria's diplomatic action and support in mediation also extended beyond the continent. With later President Abdelaziz Bouteflika as the then young Minister of Foreign Affairs, it played a mediator role in the Vietnamese Conflict. The 'Algiers Accord' settled the border disputes between Iraq and Iran in 1975, for instance, and it hosted the non-aligned movement of bloc-free states during the cold war. In the 1980s, Algeria's integrational endeavours shifted towards the Maghreb region (Mortimer, 2015). Currently, Algeria remains committed to Pan-Africanism and ranks among the highest contributors to both the AU and the Arab League — both budget-wise and in terms of staff.

To sum up, this section has given an overview of the country as an object of study. The People's Democratic Republic of Algeria holds much more than is widely known or assumed, for example, in terms of its rich history, which is still too often reduced to colonial times in Western perception. In this sense, the media in Europe and beyond mostly portray negative aspects, to the extent that they barely have any press correspondents in Algeria, a practice that is ignorant of its rich culture and diversity as well as its significant economy and its strategic geopolitical position in Africa, the Arab world, in the Mediterranean and indeed worldwide. Therefore, it is appropriate that Algeria receives the global acknowledgement due in academia, literature, and the arts, wherein the Algerian diaspora will hopefully make its contribution by taking on a more active role.

2.2   Islamic and Colonial Era

> Al-Djazair est la patrie des hommes respectueux du savoir,
> insurgés et fondateurs d'une Nation symbole. Avant 1832,
> la majorité des Algériens savait lire et écrire l'arabe. En
> 1962, l'analphabétisme concernait près de 90% du peuple.
> Le colonialisme a tenté de priver les Algériens de savoir,
> de mémoire et de les couper de leur identité culturelle[11]
> (Cherif, 2013, p. 11).

Algeria had had a long-standing tradition of education before
the arrival of French colonists in 1830[12]. In the Muslim-
Islamic tradition there had been Qu'ranic schools at first
level, *madrasas*, teaching the Qu'ran and literacy in the Arabic
language, and secondary school types – *zaouïas* in rural
and *medersas* in urban areas; religious schools providing
knowledge in Islamic literature, theology, law and history at
the secondary level (Kateb, 2014).[13] Importantly, education
was provided for and available to males only.

However, since the 14th century, the University of
Tlemcen[14] ceased to exist for as-yet unknown reasons, and
outside of intellectual circles in the principal mosques of the
main cities, there had been no formalised higher education

11   Al-Djazair [Algeria] is the homeland of the knowledge-
      loving men, insurgents and founders of a symbol Nation.
      Before 1832, the majority of Algerians knew how to read and
      write Arabic. In 1962, illiteracy affected almost 90% of the
      people. Colonialism tried to deprive Algerians of knowledge,
      memory and cut off their cultural identity.
12   See Faruqi (2006) for an account of 'Contribution of Islamic
      scholars to the scientific enterprise' and James (1954)
      Stolen Legacy for an alternative history of Greek-attributed
      philosophy originating in Egypt. See also Zeleza (2006) for
      a historical contextualisation of African universities from a
      global South perspective.
13   See primary source Turin (1971) for detailed statistics
      on primary and secondary-level education in Algeria,
      precolonial as well as 1830–1880.
14   Algerian intellectual Ibn Khaldoun had taught there. It was
      similar in its academic programmes to European medieval
      universities of the time.

in Algeria for centuries, with students being sent abroad to Islamic institutions of higher learning in Egypt, Morocco, or Tunisia, to pursue tertiary-level studies (Daghbouche, 1982; Dahmane, 2014). While Algeria was only granted its first full university from 1909 as a French public institution, both Morocco and Tunisia already had private, i.e. non-French but local-administered institutions, with religious and Arabic instruction as central elements. These institutions, El Azhar University in Cairo, Karaouyne University in Fes, and Zitouna University in Tunis, continued to be frequented by so-called 'indigenous'/*musulman* (Muslim) Algerians in the first half of the 20th century (Kateb, 2014).[15]

Concerning pre-higher education, according to Thomas Campbell (1777–1844),

> Before 1830 the Algerians were clearly more educated than the French colonisers, this historical but embarrassing truth passed over in silence and ignored by the Algerians themselves, noted by a French historian in 1830. 'All of the Algerians mastered reading, writing and 'arithmetic''. When we arrived, Campbell noted, there were over a hundred primary schools in Algiers, 86 in Constantine, 50 in Tlemcen. Algiers and Constantine each had six to seven secondary schools, and Algeria had ten zaouïa (universities). Each village had its school. Our occupation meant an irreparable blow. 10 years later Mgr Dupuch informs us that in 1840 he found only two teachers for the whole province of Algiers. 50 years later, in 1880, there were only 13 (I mean thirteen) Franco-Arab schools for all of Algeria. 'We have,' says our great orientalist George Marcais, 'been wasting this universal Muslim heritage, it was an eyesore, it was a veritable cultural extermination. Our only superiority over them is our artillery, and they

---

15   Alternatively, universities in France were frequented by a marginal number of Algerians able and willing to pursue French-modelled higher education, as early as the 19th century, as they lacked local higher education institutions.

know it. Algerians had more wit and sense than Europeans'
(...) (Habart, 2013, pp. 137–139).[16]

It is essential to highlight the discrepancy between political
discourse and the (non-)action taken, in that the colonial
doctrine espoused by Paris must be contrasted with the
concrete colonial experience in the case of Algeria. The
French colonial ideology of assimilation was supposed to be
reflected in, and implemented by, education,[17] yet from the
time of settlement until the second world war, schooling for
the local population was almost non-existent. The French
closed existing schools in the years following the occupation
and replaced them with institutions after the French model,
aimed at educating European settlers, not local people
(Ageron, 1968). There were never enough schools built for
Algerian school-age children, who had the status of so-called
'indigenous'/indigenat.[18]

The first public instruction at primary school level
was established in Algeria in 1832 and complemented by the
secondary level in 1835.[19] While free-of-charge and secular
primary education for the so-called 'non-indigenous' children

---

16   Translated from the French original by the author.
17   Cf. Heggoy (1973).
18   The Code de l'indigénat, subsuming 27 related decrees,
     was first introduced in Algiers in February 1875. It specified
     a so-called sujet/'subject' status for local populations
     (so-called indigènes/'indigenous') in French colonies and
     territories, as opposed to constitutional provisions to those
     of the occupying French citizens, European settlers, and
     Algerian Jews, who were equally granted French citizenship.
     It remained valid until after the second world war. See
     Balandier (1951) for the theoretical underpinning of the
     colonial situation of a minority achieving to subvert 90 % of
     the population.
19   See Kateb (2014) for an extensive account on the French
     colonial education system in Algeria, 1833-1962, including
     statistics. Since the focus and scope of this thesis is on
     higher education, primary and secondary-level institutions
     are not treated in more detail here. For their emergence
     and development, and a typology of the multitude of then
     existing schools, see Colonna (1975).

as French citizens became mandatory in 1883 through the law *Jules Ferry* law, this marked the end of Arab traditional schools and the beginning of two official systems of primary schooling (A/B). Simplified, system 'A' meant the French schools, providing Europeans' education, and system 'B' meant the Qu'ranic schools, delivering 'indigenous' instruction in the form of the so-called reformist religious and Algerian cultural schools, mostly in the cities, and more rural, informally organised instruction, picking up from what was left of earlier structures after the destruction by the French (Colonna, 1972). What added to the complexity of the situation was that while non-European children were in theory admissible to the 'A' stream, their enrolment remained negligible until independence,[20] even when the two streams were officially merged after the second world war.

Contrary to what the dichotomy suggests, these systems of secondary schooling co-existed and were mutually dependent on each other in colonial society. At the secondary level, the emergence of a so-called middle section, the 'indigenous' elites, was needed to manage the large population of 'subjects' vis-à-vis the very few Europeans, in what can be labelled a model of the 'correct distance principle' (Colonna, 2008).[21] This elite had to be French-speaking. Hence, for secondary education from the age of 10–12, the two pathways were continued in principle; however, there was a variety of institutions exercising the continuum of accepting versus refusing French state instruction. These ranged from the French *lycée*, leading to French universities, including in Algiers; to écoles as higher school institutions, to state-recognised *medersas* in the middle, for French colonial public administration positions; to Arab universities outside

---

20 For figures and statistics from the end of the 19th century until independence, see Colonna (2008).

21 See Colonna (2008), Table 1: 'Educational Possibilities "for the natives" in Algeria between the Jules Ferry Reform and WWII', p. 293.

of Algeria; and to rural *zaouïras* educating prospective local autonomous leaders and Qu'ranic lecturers (Colonna, 1972).[22]

Although the *medersas*[23] were established as Muslim secondary education institutions in Tlemcen, Medea (transferred to Blida and then Algiers shortly after) and Constantine by decree in 1850, they were aimed at dispensing instruction of a professional nature[24] by training assistants or mid-level civil servants for the colonial administration only, shown by the fact that they were put under military authority. Hence, directors and professors were appointed by the then French Ministry *de la Guerre* (War), following a proposal by the *Gouverneur général* (Kateb, 2014). They were integrated in the Academy of Algiers into the French public instruction system in 1876 and underwent reforms in 1895, reinforcing French-language instruction in addition to Arabic, to the detriment of theological education. From that year, too, only *medersas* graduates were admitted for Muslim civil servant recruitment in the colonial administration. Out of approximately 100 candidates taking the *concours*, the entrance examination[25] half were retained. At the beginning of the 20th century, there were about 150 students/graduates each year, with peaks of around 200 in the first decade. By 1949, there were 144 *medersas* country-wide with 40,000 students in total (Kateb, 2014) and in 1955, as many as 193 were recorded by their

---

22 See Colonna (1972), diagram on p. 211 for a graphical representation, and diagram on p.218 for an illustration of a hierarchical structure of education in colonial Algeria from primary to higher level, and associated careers.

23 See Bettahar (2008) for an inventory of primary sources on higher education in colonial Algeria available at the Archives Nationales d'Outre Mer (ANOM) in Aix-en-Provence, France.

24 This is also shown by the fact that, finally in 1951, they were transformed into lycées preparing for the baccalaureat as university entrance diploma (Kateb (2014), thus equivalent to grammar school in the system of secondary education.

25 This type of examination for admission to postgraduate studies or professional positions in civil service is the default approach in both France and Algeria.

Oulemas association; albeit with fewer students overall – 35, 150 (Pervillé, 2004).

The first Algerian teachers were therefore trained at the École Normale Supérieure (ENS) in Bouzareah, Algiers – which exists to this day – from 1883 until 1939, alongside Europeans, but in some form of 'apartheid' (Colonna, 1975). This further illustrates the fact that the objective of separation between French and Algerians was achieved in a double manner, with the latter not quite like the Europeans, yet, admitted to their institutions, the elite among the locals (Colonna, 1975). Accordingly, the concept of French higher education in the colonies[26] was to establish institutes of tertiary education covering the specific needs of the European settler society, the écoles *supérieures*, rather than to implant the system operating in Paris at the time. As early as 1832, the École de *médecine* was established, although it was only operational for four years before reopening in 1858, requiring authorisation by the French Minister *de la Guerre* for all non-French students, i.e. Maures, Turks and Jews (République Française, 1960). In that '*Elle devrait contribuer* à *la conquête des indigènes et* à *leur soumission*',[27] it had a clear-cut ideological as well as missionary function of colonial supremacy (Guerid, 2010).

The foundation for Algerian comprehensive institutional colonial higher education was then laid down by law in December 1877, separating theory-focused institutions from those with a more practical orientation (République Française, 1960). Two years later, the central library of the later University of Algiers was established, although a medical and science library had existed since 1857. Likewise, in 1880, the Écoles of *Lettres, Droit,* and *Sciences* (Schools of Literature, Law, and Science, respectively) were founded, completing all the disciplines necessary for the training of the colonial administration of so-called *France nouvelle.* These were controlled by the French state, initially financed by Paris,

---

26   See Singaravélou (2009) for an overview of higher education in former French colonies worldwide.

27   'It should contribute to the conquest of the natives and their submission.'

and complemented by the local Governor, the city of Algiers, and the three *départements* in terms of the operating budget (Bettahar, 2014). Resistance to a fully-fledged university institution in Algeria as such, however, was fierce, as there was fear of a triumph of '*l'algérianité*' over '*la francité*'[28] on the one hand, and, the '*Français de l'Algérie*' of Southern European origin, who would benefit from the institution, were considered second-class citizens in the *métropole*, on the other (Guerid, 2010). A mission by the then Higher Education Minister in 1897, assessing whether Algeria should have its own university and thus partake in the transformations in mainland France, remained without effect, as did several other delegation visits after the turn of the century.[29] Between 1879/80 and 1908/09, as few as 178 diplomas were delivered across all four écoles (Pervillé, 2004). Therefore, it took nearly eighty years from occupation until the establishment of the first comprehensive, university-type institution of higher education.

Modern-day higher education, including its postgraduate training and research mandate, in colonial Algeria, thus begins with the founding of the University of Algiers as well as its two annexes in the west of the country, Oran, and in the east, Constantine, in 1909. By this act, the former écoles were transformed into faculties of the new institution. In its early years, only law and medicine continued to be proposed for higher learning (Mélia, 1950). Within the first five years of its existence, 129 diplomas were delivered across the four faculties, among them being the first two medical degrees (Pervillé, 2004).[30] In later years, a total of 12 affiliated institutes were established, with most established only in the 1940s and even as late as the 1950s (République

28 Algerianity/Frenchness.
29 See Bettahar (2014) for historical events, actors involved, and details on the more than decade-long founding process as well as the evolution over the following decades until independence.
30 See Khelfaoui (1996) for a historical-sociological overview of the emergence of and developments in the scientific community in Algeria spanning the period 1962–1992.

Française, 1960). Not least, the modern French-colonial 'National Library of Algiers' was only inaugurated in 1958, too, after a predecessor institution dating from 1835.

In line with its ideological outset of promoting and sustaining colonialism, the university was mainly aimed at educating settlers of European origin (Ronze, 1930). Therefore, Algerian Muslim students only made up as little as approximately 3% between 1880 – then in the *écoles* – and at the university until the 1920s, and were thus practically absent. At the same time, there was emigration to Syria in particular, in order to escape from European instruction for those who could afford it – mainly financially comfortable families from the former intellectual capital Tlemcen (Bettahar, 2014). While there are insufficient and thus unreliable records, their number is estimated at a few dozen before 1914, rising to 47 in 1920, 65 in 1925 and 150 in 1935. Out of these, throughout the years, as few as seven female students were recorded; between 1936 and 1938 (Pervillé, 2004). Only from 1950 onwards was there a slight increase, although by 1954 women still accounted for a meagre 500 or 10% of the total registered at the time (Kateb, 2014). It is noteworthy that Algeria only attained full judicial independence from France at the end of 1947 through the *Statut organique de l'Algérie*, including full French citizenship and associated civil rights.

While student numbers were stagnating or declining overall, due to a preference for Paris, or the beginnings of civilian departure from Algeria due to the war situation, there was no significant change in this distribution of student numbers in the years leading up to independence (République Française, 1960; Guerid, 2010). It must be considered that, despite fluctuations, as many or more Algerian students were in France at any given time – mainly in Paris but also in places such as Montpellier and Toulouse – effectively at least doubling the numbers.

In 1960, the final year of available statistics pre-independence, 'indigenous' Algerian students accounted for 18% of a total of 7,248 students at the University of Algiers (including its annexes) (Kateb, 2014; Pervillé, 2004). However, it is noteworthy that more Algerian students studied in France at this time: a total of 1,230, in addition to 1,883 Algerian scholarship holders around the world in the academic year 1960/61, with approximately half in neighbouring Morocco and Tunisia, one quarter in the former Soviet Union, Yugoslavia and East Germany, and somewhat fewer in the USA, Switzerland and West Germany (Pervillé, 2004).

The *Fac Centrale* ('Central College') then assumed a leading role during the 1954–1962 war of independence.[31] As early as 1956, the general strike had all Algerian students[32] leave university to join the *maquis*[33] (Drif, 2013), with many never returning. In the 1940s, a majority of the nascent national movement members were graduates or advanced students at the University of Algiers, such as the former president of the *Association des* étudiants *musulmans nord-africains (AEMNA)*,[34] pharmacist Ferhat Abbas, who proclaimed the *Gouvernement de l'Algérie combattante (GPRA)*[35] in Cairo in 1958, as well as his successor Benyoucef Benkhedda during the last year of war before independence, then integrated into the

31   See Wallon (2014) for the role of the following two national student associations in the war of independence and a detailed chronology of events 1955–1962.
32   See Pervillé (2004) for a historical analysis, providing a comprehensive statistical, sociological and political account of Algerian students as well as the ideology of Muslim intellectuals, 1880–1962.
33   Algerian Resistance fighters – the political group associated with the place (name).
34   Association of North African Muslim students, to be differentiated from The Union Générale des Etudiants Musulmans Algériens (UGEMA), founded in Paris in 1955, dissolved by the French government in 1958, and subsequently operated from Lausanne and Tunis with wide international recognition. It constituted an alternative representation in contrast to the oldest student association in the world, since 1907, the Union Nationale des Etudiants de France (UNEF), which took up an ambiguous position during the war, proclaiming its support for the Algerian cause only in mid-1960.
35   'Government of Algeria in combat.'

political party *Front de la Libération Nationale (FLN)*.[36] The few Algerians who prepared and monitored the Évian *accords* – the Evian agreements, a treaty between France and the Provisional Government of the Algerian Republic, formally ending the Algerian war of independence, signed 18 March 1962 in Évian-les-Bains, France – were law or medicine graduates, too (Bedjaoui, 2018).[37] As a matter of fact, the university library was set on fire in June 1962, days before the referendum, by pro-French paramilitary organisation *Organisation de l'Armée secrète (OAS)*, destroying more than half of the 500,000 volumes in what was the second-largest collection of French libraries at the time, after the Sorbonne in Paris (Kateb, 2014).

Notably, the Evian agreements foresaw and guaranteed the continuation of French interests through cooperation, detailed as follows in Chapter II, 'Cooperation Between France and Algeria', Part B, Article 3: 'French personnel, in particular teachers and technicians, will be placed at the disposal of the Algerian Government by agreement between the two', and, in the attached *Declaration of Principles concerning Economic and Financial Cooperation*, Title 1, 'French Contribution to the Economic and Social Development of Algeria', Article 1/2 (Algeria, 1962).[38]

> In order to make a lasting contribution to the continuity of the economic and social development of Algeria, France will

---

36   National Liberation Front, Algerian political party founded at the beginning of the Algerian war for independence, which it won in 1962; former ruling party until Presidential elections in December 2019.

37   Although academics involved were not as numerous as elsewhere in independence movements, such as in the former Federation of French colonies in West Africa (Afrique-Occidentale française – AOF).

38   Reprinted from an English translation issued by the Press and Information Service, Embassy of France, New York, N.Y. The official French texts were published in the Journal Officiel of the French Republic on March 20, 1962. Cf. the French original: https://peacemaker.un.org/sites/peacemaker.un.org/files/DZ-FR_620319_AccordsEvian.pdf

2. Historical and Political Context

continue her technical assistance and preferential financial aid. For an initial period of three years, renewable, this aid will be fixed in conditions comparable to and at a level equivalent to those of programs now underway. French financial and technical aid will apply notably to the study, execution or financing of the public or private investment projects presented by the competent Algerian authorities; to the training of Algerian cadres and technicians; and to the assignment of French technicians. (...)

Hence, the presence of French was legally agreed upon for an extended period post-independence, which also included the new country's higher education system in laying the foundation for the so-called *coopération technique* by lecturers starting in the academic year 1962/63.

2.3 Independence and State-Building Era

> Avant toute chose, il faut admettre ceci: l'université algérienne d'aujourd'hui n'est pas détachable de son histoire et le poids de cette histoire continue de peser sur le présent. Jusqu' à la réforme de 1971, c'était une université libérale et élitiste, expression fidèle de la société coloniale puis de la société de l'Algérie de la première décennie de l'indépendance39 (Guerid, 2012a, p. 36).

The development of the Algerian higher education system as a whole and its individual institutions, in particular, is inextricably tied to historical events, shaping policy. Most available literature takes a historical or political approach covering post-independence to the present.

---

39   'Above all, we must admit this: the Algerian university today is not detachable from its history and the weight of this story continues to impact the present. Until the 1971 reform, it was a liberal and elitist university, a faithful expression of the colonial society, and, subsequently, of the Algerian society of the first decade of independence.'

Concluding a bloody eight-year war for independence, 1954–1962, the French *Département d'outre-mer* of the past emerged as the Democratic Republic of Algeria. The first academic year following independence, 1962/63, was marked by a student body reduced by approximately 50% to 3,817 students, more than two-thirds Algerian (Kateb, 2014) in the country's only higher education institution, the University of Algiers. With the sudden departure of the vast majority of the French population in the early 1960s, the country found itself not only with insufficient numbers of *cadres*[40] but, indeed, with almost no tertiary education instructors, with training lacking over several decades due to prior negligence by the French. Consequently, for the rest of the decade, there were many *coopérants* (development workers), both from France and, from the 1970s, increasingly, Arab countries, with Egyptian presence being most prominent. Two other universities were founded from the already existing annexes in the West and East respectively, the University of Oran (today: Oran 1 Ahmed Ben Bella), and the University of Constantine (today: Constantine 1).

Throughout the 1960s then, higher education in Algeria remained French by curricula, academic staff, diplomas, and its elite orientation, to the extent that: '*En cette période, rien ne distinguait l'université algérienne de l'université française*' (Guerid, 2007, p. 282).[41] The inherited French law regarding the university remained valid until further notice (Mahiou, 2015, p. 14), and prominent sociologists from Europe, such as Pierre Bourdieu and Jean-Claude Passeron, taught during stays in Algiers. Hence, the post-colonial university could be summed up as follows:

L'université héritée était dénoncée pour son élitisme malthusien: c'était une institution prestigieuse qui maintenait des standards élevés au niveau international, mais au prix de fortes déperditions. On lui reprochait son

---

40   Overarching term for intellectuals, leaders, executives.
41   'During this period, nothing distinguished the Algerian university from the French university.'

académisme, ses programmes abstraits et théoriques, son mépris de la formation professionnelle42 (Ghalamallah, 2006, p. 33).

In fact, only protests by students prevented the proposed simultaneous Algerian adoption of a higher education reform in France in 1965 (Guerid, 2010). Constantine and Oran as former annexes remained dependent university centres until 1969, although an Algerian École *nationale d'administration* was founded as early as 1964. Nevertheless, still in 1966, there were seven French-modelled Écoles *Nationales*, one École Normale Supérieure, two Écoles *Supérieures*, as well as seven *Instituts Nationaux*, yet, only the four historic faculties (Ministère de l'Education Nationale, 1966).

Most lecturers were French *coopérants* in the years following independence (Siino, 2014). In 1962, out of more than 30,000 that had worked in Algeria over two decades, there were 15,000 such *coopérants* in Algeria, mostly school teachers. University lecturers were far less numerous, yet occupied almost all teaching positions, and, counting 1,400, continued to do so in the majority until the 1970s (Laskaris, 2016). Urban youth, whose parents had commonly been former employees of the colonial administration such as judicial clerks or traders, made up almost the entire student body (Sidi Boumediene, 2013) at the beginning of the 1960s. At the end of the decade, there were only about 10,000 students and still fewer than 2,000 Algerian academic staff[43] at the beginning of the 1970s (Guerid, 2010). In 1970 too, only 811 university diplomas were awarded to Algerians (Kateb, 2014). Up until the early 1980s, there were 9,000 foreign lecturers, exceeding 75% of the total (Kadri & Ghouati, 2006).

---

42 'The inherited university was denounced for its Malthusian elitism: it was a prestigious institution that maintained high standards at the international level, but at a heavy trade-off. The institution was treated with contempt for its academicism, its abstract and theoretical courses, and scant regard for professional training.'

43 See Khelfaoui (2000) for an account on the development of Algerian staff framework conditions 1962–1998.

The university community thus stood in sharp contrast to the majority of Algerian youth whose socio-economic profile was predominantly rural and illiterate at the time. This situation favoured the radicalisation of the political commitment of students and executives towards a Marxist and populist ideology (Chachoua, 2015). The university campuses and especially university residences, isolated from the city, became spaces for ideological debates and sometimes violent clashes between various political groupings, such as between the arabophones and the francophones. In Algiers, back then considered as the Mecca of revolutionaries, the first groupings of the extreme left, both Marxist and Maoist, formed, as did the movement for the reclaim of the Berber identity and the Muslim brothers.

It was only in the early 1970s that a major reform was introduced, *La Refonte.* 1971 marked the year of the creation of the Algerian national university. During the dedicated press conference, the then Minister of Higher Education, Mohamed Benyahia, defined the objectives of the Algerian university, first of all, in '(...) *former les cadres, tous les cadres dont le pays a besoin*' (MESRS, 1971).[44] Given the guideline that '*Il est impérieux que l'Université se reconnaisse dans son peuple et que le peuple se reconnaisse dans son Université*',[45] he specified its training and education mission as follows :

· *Cadre engagé dans l'œuvre socialiste du pays.*
· *Cadre imprégné de la personnalité algérienne et des réalités* socio-économiques *nationales.*
· Cadre dont la formation lui permet de faire face concrètement aux problèmes spécifiques du pays.
· Cadre dont la formation scientifique garantisse un niveau permettant l'assimilation constante des progrès du patrimoine de connaissances Universelles.

---

44   '(...) train the executives, all the leaders that the country needs.'
45   'It is imperative that the University recognises itself in its people and that the people recognise themselves in their university.'

· (MESRS, 1971, pp. 12–13).[46]

The core of the reform was thus the democratisation of higher education (Djeflat, 1990, p. 37) and the concept of integration on three levels: training and teaching; structure, and nation (Benachenhou, 1980, p. 28). The first concept of 'teaching and training' refers to obtaining a position in the economic, social or technical sector after graduation. Therefore, the curriculum needed to feature both fundamental/basic knowledge and advanced, scientific knowledge units. Notably, this meant a shift from the annual colonial system of evaluation of students' learning, in place up to the 1970s, to a modular assessment system, characterised by continuous monitoring (*contrôle continu*) as the main feature of the evaluation system. Students could only pass or fail modules and gain access to a higher level if prerequisites allowed it. Since the mid-1980s, by a new university charter, an annualisation of the evaluation system was implemented, allowing students to compensate between modules and pass to the next year, which would be retained with the adoption after the Bologna Process from the early 2000s.

The second concept covers a reorganisation of the internal structure of the university according to teaching requirements rather than the individual lecturer's preferred subject matter, which implies administrative centralisation. Finally, the university was re-integrated into the society it served, instead of imposing its own abstract programmes. The university, which is itself in constant evolution, was newly shaped by the revolution as an agent of change (Benachenhou, 1980, pp. 29–35). In this context, inspired by the Anglo-Saxon model of basic and applied science, the former Faculty of

---

46   'a) Leaders engaged in the socialist work of the country.
       b) Leaders imbued with the Algerian personality and
          national socio-economic realities.
       c) A leader whose training enables him to face the specific
          problems of the country in concrete terms.
       d) Leaders whose scientific training guarantees a level
          allowing the constant assimilation of progress in the
          heritage of Universal knowledge.'

Science was split into several institutes, one for each discipline. The first university since independence – *L'Université des sciences et de la technologie Houari Boumediene* (*USTA*/from 1980 *USTHB*) was founded in 1974 on the outskirts of Algiers. In 1976, postgraduate-level education was introduced, and research first began to be institutionalised.

At the end of the 1970s, two of the French *coopérants*[47] gave an account of their experience of several years' teaching at the Algerian university. Initially wondering why Algerian students volunteered to do farm work during the Agrarian Revolution, they describe a 'technocratic' environment, yet without technology, or, indeed, the transfer of only equipment but not knowledge (Glasman & Kremer, 1978, p. 3), leading to a new dependence on foreign – technical rather than managerial – expertise in the processing industry as well as in education (Glasman & Kremer, 1978, p. 245).

Although sufficient funding was available due to flourishing fossil fuels exploitation, implementation of the reform was slow and would take another decade, due to the '*double décalage – historique et institutionnel*' (Kadri, 1991, p. 161)[48]. In a national meeting on higher education in Algiers in 1980, it was found that, despite the policy measures formally implemented according to 'Algerians living in a socialist society and keeping with the principles stated in the national plan' (Daghbouche, p. 5), still, '(…) "cooperant" teachers are used to replace Algerian assistant teachers. This action hinders the recruitment of Algerian assistant teachers and again slows down the Algerianization of staff' (Daghbouche, p. 7). It must be stressed, however, that this practice only applied where there was a shortage in specialised fields.

Overall, however, the 1980s constituted the end of the colonial legacy in the Algerian university (Lardjane, 2007). Postgraduate students were more numerous, and the number of university centres was expanded to some large cities in

---

47   See Siino (2014) for an account of lecturers in this
       framework in the Maghreb countries, 1960–1980.
48   'double shift – historical and institutional.'

the north, yet not to all other regions (MESRS, 2013). This decade was also marked by the phenomenon of university unemployment in Algeria (Benghabrit & Haddab, 2008). The university centre of Tizi-Ouzou, opened in 1977, is a symbol of this political transition from colonial university to a national and even regional university (Kadri, 1991). The capital of the Kabylia region was the scene of the first social movement and the first open demonstration in the history of independent Algeria, following the ban of a Kabyle poetry conference by the anthropologist-writer Mouloud Mammeri on March 10, 1980. This student movement became known as the *printemps berbère* ('Berber Spring') (Ait Larbi, 2010).

Ordinary young people and the sons of peasants, increasingly, were returning from Algiers, Oran, or Annaba as doctors, lawyers or engineers. These professions, formerly out of reach for the Algerian rural world, became the *métiers de rêve*[49], and thus the disciplines with the highest social prestige, reflecting the transformation from a more elitist to a socialist orientation (Guerid, 2010). Still, the post-independence *futurs-cadres-de-la-nation*, those ranked highest in their graduation class, received state-sponsored scholarships at universities in Western countries. After completing their postgraduate studies, they often returned to Algeria with a symbolic prestige, which entitled them to an executive position in the public service, academia, at one of the big national companies in fossil fuel exports, or the newly founded process engineering industries, SONATRACH (petroleum), SONELEC (electricity and electronics), or SNS (steel), as well as entitlements to government housing (Kadri, 2000).

Therefore, some senior executives who were politically active in the single party *FLN* were beginning to become part of the *bourgeoisie*, the middle class. The socio-economic crisis in 1985/86, caused by the global fall in fossil fuel prices, was followed by the revolt of October 5, 1988, a week-long street riot by the Algerian Youth, spreading to several cities around the country. The biggest protest since independence

---

49   'dream professions.'

was met with brutal regime resistance, with the military shooting at the protesters, killing some and leaving several hundred injured. The aftermath of this event indirectly ended *FLN* rule through the legalisation of political parties and non-governmental organisations (NGOs), and the lifting of press censorship (Zoubir, 2019). Furthermore, it socially impoverished university elites and, later, paved the way for fundamentalist terrorist violence after the cessation of the electoral process in the end of 1991 (Boukhobza, 1991). The leader of the largest opposition party, the *Front Islamique du Salut (FIS)*/ ('Islamic Salvation Front'), Abassi Madani, was a professor in the Department of Psychology at the University of Social Sciences in Algiers at the time. His demand for the immediate establishment of an Islamic Republic resulted in a wave of terrorism (Haroun, 2014) that developed into an atrocious civil war, today generally discreetly referred to as the *décennie noire* ('black decade').

Arguably, this past situation still has an impact on today's political set-up. Also, the departure into exile, and the subsequent move of Algerian university professors to French, other European and Canadian universities, was widespread. This cannot be compared to the so-called 'brain drain' in academia abroad as the economic situation in Algeria was comfortable for most lecturers (Guerid, 2007, p. 303). The emigrant Algerian population was approximately 1,5 million in 1990, mainly dispersed across eight OECD countries – Belgium, Canada, France, Germany, Italy, the Netherlands, Spain, and the USA. The annual exodus remained at around 20,000 until 2000, when it suddenly doubled (Natter, 2020)[50].

Students, even in the early 1990s, were conscious of the likelihood of being unemployed (Guerid, 2007, pp. 292–293) as a side-effect of the now prevailing massification of higher education. Although national scientific activity came to an almost complete standstill during the Black decade, several institutional policies were implemented, among them, in

---

50   Notably, these figures have remained constant since. See also Natter (2014).

1991–1992, the creation of so-called university centres of excellence, in 1995 the creation of regional academies (Centre, East, West), and, in 1999, the integration of information and communication technology (ICT). The *Conférence nationale des universités (CNU)*, consisting of the three regional conferences (Centre, West, and East) was founded in 2001.

2.4 Contemporary Era

The 2000s saw the rise of fuel prices and, with the arrival of a president serving from 1999 to 2019, Abdelaziz Bouteflika, a 1970s reprise of higher education politics, wherein he was a major actor. Although under different circumstances, and influenced by an ever-growing population, a liberal economy, a multi-party system, and information technology, his policy of *concorde civile* ('social harmony') has, in fact, once again supported a massive construction of universities in each *Wilaya* (regional administrative unit).

With student numbers at half a million in the academic year 2000/2001, this marks an impressive increase of 1,000% from just 500 in 1954 (Guerid, 2010). The policy allowed first-generation students to access university education and, above all, gain a feeling of socioeconomic success through ascension and modernisation, as well as individual empowerment, leading to social harmony (Merzouk, 2012). Combined with the successive adoption of the EU-initiated Bologna Process of higher education harmonisation[51] across participating countries from 2003 onwards, Algeria has reached greater inclusivity in first- and second-level education and opened up the university to the broader population, newly covering the interior regions in the South, as well as a growing female participation, constituting the majority nowadays, and surpassing male numbers for the first time in 2005. By the end of 2010, student numbers already exceeded one million.

---

51   Locally, and in francophone contexts, generally referred to as the LMD (system).

However, given the background of slow implementation of reforms from decades ago, it is equally not surprising that it is asked: 'Why do we have to stick to any French educational system?' (Daghbouche, 2011, p. 468). Higher education, according to a highlighted contribution in Ghalamallah's edited collection, occupies a primary role in the reproduction of the social structure and may present an opportunity for a different one indeed (Derguini, 2011, p. 117). A second contribution proposes, in terms of measuring efficiency and effectiveness, '*objectifs de démocratisation, d'arabisation, d'algérianisation et de scientificité*'[52] (Bakouche, 2011, p. 165). Likewise, Guerid exposes an 'emprunt culturel' in the policy of industrialisation, which is regarded, and, as adopted, as Western universal model without '*une réflexion profonde sur l'université nationale à construire*'[53] (Guerid, 2012a, pp. 41–42). This state of affairs points towards the necessity of historical contextualising as well as its influence up to today. Nevertheless, Guerid claims that there is an '(…) *absence d'une stratégie consensuelle et à long terme et partant d'une définition claire de l'université et de sa mission, dans la non-*émergence *d'un contre-pouvoir académique*'[54] (Guerid, 2010).

Indeed, Guerid sees the underlying issue in the fact that there exists no knowledge society in Algeria as of now: '*Est-il possible de construire une université de savoir dans une société qui n'est pas une société du savoir ni dans la réalité ni en projet?*'[55] (Guerid, 2012a, p. 34). From a comparative perspective, 'the Algerian university aims to serve the society's needs, serve the scientific researches and seeks to adapt the technological

---

52   'Objectives of democratisation, arabisation, algerianisation and scientificity.'
53   cultural imprint – 'A deep reflection on the national university to be built.'
54   '(…) absence of a consensual and long-term strategy and therefore of a clear definition of the university and its mission, in the non-emergence of an academic counter-power.'
55   'Is it possible to build a university of knowledge in a society that is not a knowledge society, neither in reality nor in planning?'

development [sic]', the description of which is portrayed as a combination of other major nations' higher education systems:

> (...) while the German university regards that the university's objective is looking for knowledge and science, the French university considers it to be serving the national and regional spirit, contrary to the Russian university which sees the main aim of the university is to fulfil the essential needs of the society, however; the American one sees that the university's objective is serving markets which are subject to competition and development, unlike the Algerian university's objective which is a mixture of the previous ideas and prospects, something that is clear in the official speeches, recommendations and practical instructions [sic] (Benaissa, 2017, English abstract).

Currently, though, an increasingly pressing reality is graduate unemployment, with its adverse impact on society's social cohesion, in addition to a generally lower level of competence and, consequently, so-called 'brain drain' (Cherif, 2013, pp. 30–31). The root cause, portrayed as the massification of the system by ever-increasing student numbers. The considerable increase in not only student numbers but higher education establishments since 2000, or even since 2010, has led to the orientation of new, especially female students, towards fields of study available at local universities, rather than moving away, and thus the governance-induced promotion of the creation of 'élites' locales' (Haddab, 2014, p. 226).

By 2010, too, the overall degradation of their social status in society had many lecturers and professors leave university for either the private sector or public administration, or indeed emigrate altogether (Guerid, 2010). Presently, due to the recent shortage of supervisory and teaching staff, young, low-skilled and inexperienced graduates are being recruited. The academic staff is made up to a large extent of lecturers in their thirties, mostly doctoral candidates or young PhD holders.

Although in 2006, in the framework of revised public sector laws, academic staff salaries were significantly increased – after being among the lowest internationally for decades – this change only applied to those with *fonctionnaire*, i.e., civil servant, status, while excluding the increasing numbers of *vacataires* (temporary as well as permanent contract holders). The teaching profession, in general, is beset by hierarchical challenges, as well as the desire to climb the professional ladder to obtain professor rank, rather than remaining at the level of (assistant) lecturer with less social benefits. Alternatively, incumbents seek to receive a promotion as an administration executive in the form of Head of Department, Dean, Vice-Dean, Vice-Rector, Head of Master's programmes or Graduate Schools, or member of administrative or scientific councils.

Consequently, as claimed by one of the country's most prominent social sciences representatives, as early as 2010 a new era of the Algerian university was about to begin, entailing the *passage de l'impératif quantité à l'impératif qualité* [56] (Guerid, 2010), i.e., a shift from a quantitative, number-focused orientation, towards a qualitative orientation. While the Algerian university is still the principal means of maintaining the status quo of the elite, the way in which this process is taking place is entirely absent from the public debate, as are other discussions about decisions in national policy fields. This state of affairs results in a lack of societal consensus on the mission of the university (Guerid, 2010).

2.5 Conclusion: The Co-Existence of the Local and the Global in Algerian Higher Education

Local Elements

One of the most recent publications, titled 'The role of the university in the development of the society' suggests that, 'The university is regarded as the most important social

---

56   change from the imperative of quantity to the imperative of quality.

institution that influences and is influenced by the social environment around it'; furthermore, there exist the functions of training 'artistic, professional, political and intellectual leaders' (Barini, 2018, English abstract). At its foundation, therefore, a country's national higher education system is an expression of the institutional system and the nature of the relationship between the state and the individual, group and society in its entirety (Derguini, 2011, p. 101).[57] Since independence, Algerian higher education policy emphasised, in continuous 5-year national development plans, and, 'based on the principle of state guidance in the supply of trained personnel' (Daghbouche, 1982, p. 10), '(…) the quantitative rather than the qualitative side of education' (Daghbouche, 2008, p. 73). This emphasis has repercussions on '(…) an adequate capacity to respond to the requirements of the new generation', meaning its ability to adapt to 21st-century challenges.

Overall, there exists the present-day dilemma of how to adapt to society on the one hand, and, at the same time, how to adapt society to the requirements of knowledge, while reconciling excellence with massification, as well as affirming that the society needs to be built on knowledge and competence (Cherif, 2013, pp. 6–7). Accordingly, although in principle everything is possible if the overall vision of the institution is agreed upon, balanced and open, the development of the university is linked to the type of governance, both nationally and internationally (Cherif, 2013, p. 7). While governance is understood broadly as encompassing both external aspects such as the relationship between the state, private sector, and civil society actors and internal elements, it is in management that problems of weak institutional capacities persist (Ghalamallah, 2011a, pp. 6–7). This situation presents itself as a paradox in a socialist state.

From a non-political background, scholar Mohamed Ghalamallah – then based at the University of Oran, and

---

57   The discussion of the relationship between society and
      university is science-intrinsic. Therefore, the discourse is
      subject to change over time. In addition, there exist several
      aspects, which may go beyond these specific expressions.

currently at *CREAD* – reflects about the Algerian university's mission and its associated functions. Referring to history, he identifies three main functions, namely, economical, critical, and, educational and cultural (Ghalamallah, p. 1). The latter two are of traditional ideological nature, in social and cultural conservation. In contrast, the first-mentioned is modern and includes the training of *cadres*, national executives and leaders (Ghalamallah, pp. 9–10). According to him, the university exists between the two pillars of exercising autonomy and academic freedom, and assuming social responsibility (Ghalamallah, pp. 7–8). This translates into its mission of research versus the pressure of social determinisms (Ghalamallah, p. 15).

In more general terms, the university has two principal missions, firstly, academic training aimed at employability, and, secondly, research (Ghalamallah, 2011b, p. 50). Consequently, strategic decisions must be made in contemporary times: should the university be oriented towards economic requirements, and train its students accordingly, or, in contrast, should the university favour critical thinking and research freedom? (Cherif, 2013, p. 47). In contrast, in an exemplary national journal article, the contemporary Algerian university is attributed a national unity function in terms of stability and social cohesion, as well as its norm-giving value for individual, collective and international relations (Hayesh & Boubaker, 2016, French abstract). Another, new function proposed is the university's role in innovation, which in turn favours economic growth (Boumediene & Beddi, 2015, pp. 31-32).

While their predominantly national context can characterise these functions, it is acknowledged that human resources in the sense of teaching and training could not have been achieved without foreign universities as a form of broad international cooperation. The international aspect of the Algerian university is thanks to its geographical position between Africa, the Arab world and Europe, '*au carrefour des cultures*'[58], of which the membership in the respective associations of universities – as early as the 1990s – is proof (Djeflat, 1990, pp. 37–40).

Overall, the Algerian national university's relationship to society as the central element has not been clarified or applied to date, as 'The main problem is how the present system can respond purposefully to the development and needs of Algerian society itself and promote the direct participation of universities in economic, social and cultural level' (Daghbouche, 2008, p. 73). According to Daghbouche (Daghbouche, 2008, p. 82), as a result of these observations, the governance aspects of the dominating rigid university system and structure are at the core of social demands versus workforce needs, while maintaining systematic links between higher and secondary education, and between employment, overall national planning, scientific research and society in general.

Global Elements

In the past, international aspects of academia embodied by research practice played a negligible role, due to heavy teaching loads; 'Thus the research situation has been adversely affected by the teaching and development role which the community has given the university', which, again, translates into the need for 'rational planning of the teaching/research functions of the universities' (Daghbouche, 1982, p. 52). As for research as a function, the university should advocate a generalist, multi-disciplinary education in science over a purely technical one in the form of vocational professional training (Ghalamallah, p. 12), and consistently expand its knowledge by resisting demands from the environment and focusing on '*valeurs d'objectivité, d'universalité, d'humanisme [comme] un instrument d'engagement (...)*'[59] (Ghalamallah, p. 17). These statements present not least a plea for research

---

58   'at the crossroads of cultures.'
59   'Values of objectivity, universality, humanism [as] an instrument of commitment (...)'

and science, subsumed under the 'critical spirit' as the central functions of the (modern) university.

Recently, the state has been reacting to quality issues (University World News/Algérie Press Service, 2018). It has successfully begun to participate in prestigious internationally competitive and selective higher education cooperation projects and institutions, such as the 'Academy' project funded by the European Union's INTRA-AFRICA academic mobility scheme coordinated by the University of Tlemcen, the United Nations University Institute for Sustainable Development (UNU-IRADDA) in Algiers in 2016, and the Pan-African University Institute of Water and Energy Sciences (including Climate Change) (PAUWES) in Tlemcen, since 2014. In September 2018, foreign private and international higher education providers were permitted to operate in Algeria for the first time, and some academies and institutes with a focus on economics, management, or elements of foreign-language instruction have since emerged. The Higher Arab Institute of Translation (HAIT) was inaugurated by the Arab League as early as 2005.

Regarding quality assurance, which relies on often supra-national standardisation and certification, the *LMD* has recently been included in the state publisher's *Office des publications universitaires (OPU)* books stock (Baddari & Herzallah, 2014); this may be regarded as evidence of its significance and topicality in scientific discourse. The significant past and continuing contribution of Algerian diaspora scholars – many of whom emigrated in the 1990s during the so-called 'black decade' of political unrest – around the world must be acknowledged. Nevertheless, as of 2015, some 54,000 academic staff of various ranks (*Direction Générale de la Recherche Scientifique et du Développement Technologique* [DGRSDT], 2015) at the country's higher education institutions are almost exclusively Algerian nationals, at 99,7% in the 2005/2006 academic year (Guerid, 2010).[60] This status quo runs counter to the global trend of

---

60   More recent statistics could not be obtained.

increasing faculty internationalisation, enabled by active recruitment and incentive policies.

Nevertheless, Algerian universities are hardly visible in the international arena as, in addition to low research output, they currently rank low down both in worldwide and regional comparisons. While international rankings must be treated cautiously in terms of, among other things, their methodology and their often inherently Anglo-Saxon as well as English-language bias, the 2019 Times Higher Education Universities World Ranking edition includes five Algerian institutions, of which two are ranked at the 800-1000th position and three at 1001+. In this classification, among African universities, these perform well in occupying the 17th-30th places, but only one appears, at 25th position, in the 2018 Arab World ranking (Times Higher Education World Universities Ranking, 2019). Out of close to 11,000 co-authored publications involving Algerian researchers analysed in 2000–2011, about 42% were written with co-authors from France, with only 3% from the United States, 2% from the United Kingdom, and less than 1,5% each from Canada, Tunisia and Morocco (DGRSDT, 2015).

As in other Arab countries, Algerian scholars, too, are among the two-thirds reported who would like to emigrate, according to a recent study in the region (University World News, 2019). The Algerian higher education system has also been increasingly subjected to external pressure, mainly by an – even if indirect – emigration trend by its graduate students, who enrol in French universities through the French public agency Campus France, established in 2010, which promotes France as a destination to pursue higher education. Hence, a significant number of Algerian graduates are striving to go to Europe or North America – not primarily to study, but to emigrate (Chachoua, 2018). Prior direct ministerial authorisation is required for institutions providing invitation letters to all foreign nationals needing a visa for academic stays in Algeria, as Algerian researchers need to equally obtain approval by the authority for the same purpose abroad. The authors' own experience of obtaining a visa shows that there is, to date, no policy of openness.

Students have also been participating actively in the so-called *hirak* movement of weekly street protests since February 2019, initially demanding the resignation of former President Abdelaziz Bouteflika, which took place in April 2019, during a month-long university closure to prevent civil action upsurge (Bensouiah, 2019a). These protests have continued to demand the continued renewal of the countries' leadership on all levels. Since delayed elections in mid-December 2019, resulting in a new government headed by the independent President Abdelmadjid Tebboune, demonstrations have become less well attended, although they do continue. Most topically, with the arrival of a new Minister of Higher Education and Scientific Research in January 2020, lecturers have voiced their demands for improved salaries, working conditions, and living allowances. Their further demands are to discontinue the reformed *LMD* system in favour of the bachelor degree system, and to switch to English and abandon French as the language of instruction (Bensouiah, 2020b).

In this context, it is noteworthy that Algerian lecturers' salary level is at a minimum of DZD 126,000/month (USD 980), with the maximum being DZD 412,000 (USD 3,200); the average is DZD 262,000 (USD 2,000). Compared internationally, this is around one-third of lecturers' salaries in some central European countries, and a maximum of one-fourth of Northern European, British, North American, Australian, and South African averages.[61].With regards to overall salary rates in other African countries, as well as the BRICS (Altbach et al., 2013), Algerian conditions compare favourably. Increases are in place after 2, 5, 10, 15 and 20 years of service, with progression percentages decreasing from 40 to 10 over time.[62] While many receive state/university accommodation as well, living costs have risen sharply,

---

61   Source:https://naibuzz.com/10-countries-with-the-highest-professor-salaries-in-the-world/
62   Source:http://www.salaryexplorer.com/salary-survey.php?loc=4&loctype=1&job=6259&jobtype=3

and only very few benefit from the highest levels, i.e., the professorial rank.[63] Those rates have not changed since 2008.[64]

To conclude, within 50 years, the Algerian higher education system has grown from a marginalised minority to an overwhelming majority of student youth, and from one single university to a large system incorporating more than a hundred institutions of various types. It not only surpassed but indeed replaced the colonial university with its national university. Finally, since the turn of the millennium, the Algerian university – while partly imposed for competitive, economic reasons due to globalisation as well as domestic civil pressure – has featured an increasingly liberal orientation. Nevertheless, it finds itself in an impasse between this international environment and its domestic traditions, with its foundations still insufficiently rooted, and saddled with a language policy that is newly challenged by the gradual introduction of English (Bettahar, 2014). Consequently, Algeria is currently at a crossroads. While potential and promising developments can be identified, there are many open questions in higher education policy, and in institutional and system development. Therefore, a rationale has to be defined with regards to priorities to be tackled.

---

63   See chapter 3.2.
64   See http://www.esrsalg.yolasite.com/resources/Version2_ Nvelle_grille_salaires.pdf for a comprehensive compilation by the Algerian National Council of Higher Education Lecturers (CNES) as an overview of all ranks, categories, and differentiation between base salary and a variety of bonuses to be added, among others, teaching, research, and region. Again, these are most relevant for the higher ranks as opposed to the lower ones.

3. Algerian Higher Education System Development

3.1 University Landscape

Algerian higher education governance at the national level is organised via the central authority of the MESRS,[1] established in 1971, after having been incorporated post-independence in the Ministry of National Education. At present, it encompasses nine General Directorates, one of which is the Directorate of Scientific Research and Technological Development *(DGRSDT)* outlined below. As stipulated by law, the Minister is appointed by the President. The Ministry has its own publication, the *Bulletin Officiel*, which appears every trimester. The most recent edition is 733 pages long.[2] It also makes available a compilation of laws governing the sector spanning the period 2005–2019 on its website (MESRS, 2019). It has also been operating its own publishing house since 1973, the *OPU*,[3] which, as a public entity, features academic books across the spectrum of disciplines, for use at university or individual scientific work.[4]

As of January 2020, the Algerian higher education system includes 106 institutions, in 58 *Wilayas* as administrative units, comprising 50 universities, 13 university centres, 20 écoles *nationales supérieures*, 10 écoles *supérieures*, 11 écoles *normales supérieures* and 2 annexes. Of these institutions, about 30% of the universities and 90% of the university centres were founded since 2000 (MESRS, 2019). These are divided into

---

1   Like its French counterpart, governance structure has been centralised.
2   https://bit.ly/4e7t0zk (Arabic only).
3   https://www.opu-dz.com/portal/fr
4   Those are much more affordable than commercial publishers by international standards. However, they are generally not exported, and foreign authors are rather unlikely to publish with them, so it essentially reflects research being done domestically.

three regions, namely, Centre (11 universities), East (22) and West (17), each with a governing body, the regional conference of universities. No conference has been established for the Algerian South yet.

The legal basis for university status of an institution is to be gazetted in the (*Journal Officiel*) *Décret exécutif n° 03-279 du 24 Joumada Ethania 1424 correspondant au 23 août 2003 fixant les missions et les règles particulières d'organisation et de fonctionnement de l'université,*[5] as well as its amendment 2007.[6] Higher education institutions are defined as 'public establishments of scientific, cultural, and professional character', where the distinction is made between 'public establishments of administrative character',[7] such as the *oeuvres universitaires*, and the 'public establishments of industrial and commercial character', such as the *OPU* as service providers. This was the first law concerning universities made since 1999[8] and stipulates their status as created by, and under the tutelage of, the Ministry. Primarily, the latter decides about their capacity, number and nature of faculties, and eventual annexes. Any alternations are subject to the same conditions.

Institutional governance is regulated by a number of Ministerial decrees dating from between 2004 and 2006, which for universities and university centres, in addition to Rectorate and general administration,[9] stipulate the following self-administration: Institute council and scientific council,

---

5   https://www.joradp.dz/JO2000/2003/051/F_Pag.htm pp. 4-13.
6   https://www.joradp.dz/JO2000/2006/061/F_Pag.htm
7   Cf. Chapter II: Dispositif institutionnel et organisationnel du secteur de l'enseignement supérieur et de la recherche scientifique, Section II, B 1) a) https://www.mesrs.dz/fr/chapitre2
8   https://services.mesrs.dz/DEJA/Ensemble%20 des%20textes%20juridiques%20depuis%20 l%27ind%C3%A9pendance%20et%20publie%20dans%20 le%20journa%20officiel%20/loi99-05fr.pdf
9   https://services.mesrs.dz/DEJA/fichiers_sommaire_des_textes/55%20FR.PDF, pp. 15–21

Faculty council and scientific council, and Department scientific council.[10] For écoles, the scientific council and its administration were legally established only in 2018.[11]

Écoles, modelled after the French type,[12] are highly selective institutions of higher education aimed at training the national elite, often with employment guaranteed in various public administrations upon graduation in their respective fields. Their legal reference is as recent as 2016.[13] Although the historical annexes in Constantine and Oran continue to be essential centres in the Algerian higher education landscape, with several universities in each city, Algerian students from any of the country's now 58 *Wilayas*, as regional administration units, including much less densely populated regions in the Algerian Sahara, now have a higher education institution of either university or university centre status nearby.

While the conditions had already been set in 1999 and updated in 2008,[14] finally, since the end of 2016, private institutions of higher education are formally permitted by ministerial decree. This constitutes a novelty as, since independence, there have only ever been public universities in Algeria, in contrast to its neighbours Morocco and Tunisia who, despite their much smaller sizes and population, are host to several private institutions – among them branch campuses of foreign universities. Although there is no private comprehensive university in Algeria yet – a dozen business-school type specialised institutions do exist – operations are expected to start in the near future and have the potential to mark the beginning of a new era in the Algerian higher

---

10   Cf. Chapter II, Section II, B 1. 1) b) Organisation scientifique des établissements. https://www.mesrs.dz/fr/chapitre2

11   https://services.mesrs.dz/DEJA/fichiers_sommaire_des_textes/57%20BIS%20%20FR.pdf pp.12–15

12   Their structure and internationally distinct type of higher education institution is identical with the French system.

13   https://www.mesrs.dz/documents/12221/3751967/n%C2%B0%2016-176.pdf/06c0d6fb-c9e9-478d-890e-3102757f0d6f

14   https://services.mesrs.dz/DEJA/fichiers_sommaire_des_textes/50%20FR.PDF, pp.33–37.

education system. To complete the Algerian higher education landscape, provision has also been made for institutions not to be under the tutelage of the respective Ministry, but other Ministries.[15] There are also national technical and vocational training Institutes, such as the *Institut Algérien du Pétrole (IAP)*. Although institutions and industries fund them, they are pedagogically dependent on the Ministry of Higher Education and Scientific Research for the accreditation of their academic programmes.

The 2018 operating budget[16] for higher education and scientific research was 313 billion Algerian dinars, equalling around USD 2.65 billion, corresponding to approximately 7% of the entire annual national budget (Ministère des Finances, 2018). This amount was used to finance all institution administration, infrastructure, teaching, and research – including those national research centres attached to the Ministry – as well as students' social services, via the Ministerial agency *Office National des Oeuvres Universitaires (ONOU)*,[17] which made up a large part of the expenses. All budget items were 98% funded by fossil fuel export revenues, in accordance with the Algerian national budget. This status quo is testimony to one of the most significant investments in any national higher education system in recent times. It constitutes a remarkable, increasing achievement of higher education access at the same time.

In the academic year 2019/2020, the Algerian higher education system included some 2 million students and more than 55,000 academic staff – including professors/researchers and doctoral candidates – (DGRSDT, 2019a) out of a population of 43.5 million. For comparison, Nigeria, the

---

15   Cf. Chapter III, Section III La formation supérieure hors du secteur de l'enseignement supérieur. https://www.mesrs. dz/fr/chapitre3 France has the same governance structure, e.g. the École Nationale des Beaux-Arts is under the guidance of the Ministry of Culture.

16   Newest available figures

17   The French equivalent is the Centre régional des œuvres universitaires et scolaires (CROUS).

most populous country in Africa, presently has similar student numbers,[18] as does South Africa, with Egypt and Germany, both double the Algerian population, each having 2.8 million students. By 2030, as many as 3 million students are expected to be enrolled at Algerian universities nation-wide, as per the opening speech on the occasion of the new Minister's inauguration (MESRS, 2020d).

According to data from UNESCO, in 2018, the Algerian – like the Chinese – tertiary education gross enrolment ratio[19] was at just over 50%, of which almost two-thirds were female. It has continually risen from 30% in 2010. The first-degree gross graduation rate was at just under 30% in 2018, which remained almost unchanged compared to 2012. Since 2010, female graduates have outnumbered their male counterparts by one-third or more (United Nations Educational, Scientific and Cultural Organisation [UNESCO], 2020). For comparison, tertiary enrolment rates are at 28% in India, 35% in Egypt – similar to the Arab States average – 22% in South Africa, and 9% for other sub-Saharan African countries, in contrast to Europe's and North America's combined 77% (UNESCO)/ Institute for Statistics, 2020a). Organisation of Economic Cooperation and Development (OECD) countries' tertiary education attainment rate – men and women combined – is around 35% on average. However, figures vary widely from under 10% (South Africa) to close to 70% (Russia and Korea) (Organisation of Economic Cooperation and Development [OECD], 2020).

---

18 https://www.pulse.ng/communities/student/national-universities-commission-nuc-says-there-are-1.9m-students-in-nigerian/3tgpcd7
19 Number of students enrolled in a given level of education, regardless of age, expressed as a percentage of the official school-age population corresponding to the same level of education. For the tertiary level, the population used is the 5-year age group starting from the official secondary school graduation age. See http://uis.unesco.org/en/glossary-term/gross-enrolment-ratio

All *baccalauréat (bac)*[20] holders have access to 100% publicly-financed institutions, and, via the Ministerial agency *ONOU*, will receive accommodation in university residences for a nominal fee, on the condition that they live further than 30 km (for female students) and 50 km (for male students) away from their place of study. In addition, there is only a token price for catering on campus, with meals costing 1,2 Algerian dinars, equalling USD 0.01 each, on restaurant ticket booklets, as well as transport for 135 dinars or USD 1,11/year. Not least, most students, depending on parental income, receive a modest stipend for associated costs, which makes Algeria one of the few, if not the only, remaining country in the world that grants not only tuition-free studies – as is also the case in all continental European countries – but also fully finances living costs for the duration of first (bachelor), second (master's) and even third-level (doctoral) courses for all domestic and foreign students.

The latter group is hosted generally via bilateral government agreements with some sub-Saharan African countries, although they only made up 0.7% of the total registered stipend receivers in 2017. In the 2017/2018 academic year, close to half a million students were accommodated in public student residences, approximately 925,000 received a stipend and campus transport, and more than 1,155,000 meals were dispensed per day (MESRS/ONOU, 2020).[21] These conditions of 95% national subsidy benefits, coupled with the unchanged, much lower price level of the time, for the costs borne by students themselves, have remained unchanged since the 1970s.

With student numbers still rising, student selection and allocation, too, is an 'instrument' of higher education policy with clearly defined economic and social objectives (Haddab, 2014, p. 232). Accordingly, in the 2018/2019 academic year, for example, postgraduate (master's and doctoral level)

---

20   Default secondary school leaving diploma in Algeria - A-level equivalent - granting university access.
21   Newest figures available.

access has been portrayed as highly problematic in terms of transparency and functionality of application processes and the disparity between over-subscribed cities and the less populated towns in the country (Bensouiah, 2018b). Since 1995, selectivity in the form of average *bac* marks[22] for popular, socially prestigious and highly sought-after disciplines like medicine, sciences, engineering, architecture and foreign languages has increased, while those with the lowest grades are generally allocated to the social sciences by a centrally administered national allocation system, which accounts for up to three-quarters of the student distribution.

According to an article in the student supplement in the 'El Watan' national newspaper, the current dominance of social sciences and humanities, catering to approximately two-thirds of all Algerian students, is not out of choice but can indeed be traced back to a lack of alternatives related to lower marks in the *bac*, limiting access to medicine, science, and engineering, for which higher grades are required (Staïfi, 2013). Not least, at the beginning of the academic year 2018/2019, the former Minister of Higher Education, Tahar Hadjar, announced that Political Science would be discontinued at 13 universities due to students' lack of interest and poor employment opportunities – although journalism as political and information science was previously only offered at one national institute – with lecturers being integrated into law faculties (Bensouiah, 2018a).

Contrary to this claim is the analysis put forward by a previous Minister of Higher Education, Mustapha Haddab, who stated that the so called STEM (Science, Technology, Engineering and Mathematics) disciplines – basically aimed at a career in academia – accounted for less than 15% of all graduates in 2005, largely due to the fact that they do not foresee remaining at university, given the low overall requirement of their profile (Haddab, 2014, pp. 229–230). SONATRACH, the biggest national enterprise engaged in petroleum engineering, has reacted to the general lack

---

22   As is the case in France.

of competence of recruited graduates with a one-year 'induction' practical training course (Guerid, 2007, p. 306). Consequently, a shift can be detected away from basic research and productivity-oriented STEM disciplines, towards a service industry with courses in management, business, communication and law now dominating the overall study structure (Haddab, 2014, p. 231).

After the adoption of Tamazight in 2016 as the second official language in Algeria, in addition to modern standard Arabic, the first signs of a shift in policy can be seen by the decree for the creation of an Algerian Academy for Tamazight Language as of June 2018, followed by a commission set up at the African Union from November 2019 (University World News/Algérie Press Service, 2019).

3.2   Research System

The Algerian science education system is comparatively recent, although its former agencies, the National Organisation for Scientific Research *(ONRS)* and the National Research Commission *(CNR)* were established shortly after *La Refonte* – with the creation of the respective Ministry – in 1972 and 1973, respectively. From 1962 until 1972, the Office of Scientific Cooperation *(ONS)* was co-administered with the French institution (Dahmane, 2014). Importantly, in 1976, the Institute of post-graduation at universities was established, corresponding to the cycle of studies post-first (*licence*-bachelor) level, and eventually having local staff, still rare in the 1980s, at the disposal of students, for both research and academic training. In 1986, following the dissolution of the *ONRS*, the High Commission of Research *(HCR)* was founded, which re-centralised research under the Presidency (Dahmane, 2014). In 1989, a national committee of programming and evaluation of scientific research *(CNEPRU)* was established,[23] and 1999 marks the beginning of the regulations of national research centres as statute type 'public

---

23   https://services.mesrs.dz/DEJA/fichiers_sommaire_des_ textes/23%20FR.PDF

establishment of scientific and technological character'[24], modified twice, in 2002 and 2009.

While the first five-year plan started in 1998 with the integration of lecturers-researchers at universities in research units, it was only ten years later that institutionalisation in the form of overarching governing agencies took place (DGRSDT, 2019a). The legal reference of present-day scientific research and technological development is the corresponding 'orientation law' from December 2015. In the overview of laws governing the sector (MESRS, 2019), those addressing and concerned with research development appear mostly from 2016 onwards, such as the creation of new national research centres.[25] Importantly, the Algerian Academy for Science and Technology[26] was only established in 2015, too, by presidential decree. Likewise, the Algerian Academy for Tamazight Language dates from 2018.

In terms of research governance, the *Direction Générale de la Recherche Scientifique et du Développement Technologique (DGRSDT)* is the national central agency attached to the Ministry, legally founded in 2008, which is charged with consolidating the national science system, research programming and evaluation, finance, scientific human resources development, scientific cooperation, and research promotion.[27] Importantly, it hosts the secretariat and executes the decisions of the national council of scientific and technical

---

24   Cf. Chapter II, Section II, Cadre institutionnel et organisationnel de l'enseignement supérieur et de la recherche scientifique. B. 1. 3) 1) a) https://www.mesrs.dz/fr/chapitre2

25   See the complete list:http://atrst.dz/en/etablissements-de-recherche/

26   Cf. Chapter II, Section II, Cadre institutionnel et organisationnel de l'enseignement supérieur et de la recherche scientifique. A) 2) 1. https://www.mesrs.dz/fr/chapitre2

27   France features a similar structural set-up as Directorate-General within the Ministry: https://www.enseignementsup-recherche.gouv.fr/cid24148/www.enseignementsup-recherche.gouv.fr/cid24148/direction-generale-de-la-recherche-et-de-l-innovation-d.g.r.i.html

research *(CRNSDT)* – last amended in 2008 after creation in 1992 – and it implements the respective national policy as stipulated by orientation law in 1998, for four years initially.[28]

In 1992, 10 intersectoral commissions of research support, programming and evaluation were installed[29], modified in 2008 and complemented by permanent, standing sector committees in 1999.[30] There are five national thematic research agencies,[31] established in 2012 with revised governing laws in 2019, aimed at basic research and overseeing 38% of research entities in the field of social sciences and humanities; 7% in natural and life sciences; 6% in biotechnologies and food processing sciences; 44% in science and technologies, and 5% in health sciences (DGRSDT, 2019b). In addition, targeted at applied research, there is a stand-alone national agency for the validification of research results and technological development *(ANVREDET)*,[32] which has existed since 1998, and the Algerian Space Agency *(ASAL)*,[33] founded by presidential decree in 2002. Accordingly, the national council for scientific research and technological development was established in 2008, followed by the national council of evaluation in 2010.[34]

Research funding as gross domestic expenditure on research and development – for which the latest, and only, figures are available 2017 – adds up to 0,5% of the GDP, of which 50% is spent on government, 43% on higher education and 6% on business. Government, with 93%, is the source of

---

28   http://www.dgrsdt.dz/Pdf/Documents/Loi_98-11_du_22-09-1998.pdf
29   https://services.mesrs.dz/DEJA/fichiers_sommaire_des_textes/77%20FR.PDF, pp.111/112.
30   https://services.mesrs.dz/DEJA/fichiers_sommaire_des_textes/78%20FR.PDF, pp.3/4.
31   Unlike in France, with its Centre National de la Recherche Scientifique (CNRS), there is no overarching, multidisciplinary research institution to which units or laboratories are affiliated.
32   https://www.anvredet.org.dz/
33   https://asal.dz/
34   https://services.mesrs.dz/DEJA/fichiers_sommaire_des_textes/20%20FR.PDF/ https://services.mesrs.dz/DEJA/fichiers_sommaire_des_textes/18%20bis%20fr.pdf

the overwhelming majority of funds. Roughly half is spent on engineering and technology, with approximately 2% each on natural sciences, medical sciences and social sciences. The remainder, more than 40%, is 'not specified' (UNESCO)/ Institute for Statistics, 2020b).

The budget for research and development indicated stands at more than 100 billion Algerian dinars, the equivalent of USD 814 million. Starting in 1997, approximately two-thirds of the total has been allocated to universities, 28% to agencies and national research centres under *MESRS* tutelage, and the remaining 6% to those outside of the latter Ministry. However, there has been a decline in overall funds since the peak in 2014, for both operational budget and equipment (DGRSDT, 2019a). A further differentiation, e.g., regarding institutions or single units, cannot be obtained.

As of 2020, the Algerian higher education system features 26 national research units[35] at universities and 25 research centres under the tutelage of *MESRS* and seven other Ministries, as well as more than 1,500 groups (*laboratoires*)[36] at universities, up from only 262 with a total of 13,150 researchers (including doctoral candidates) in 2000, their year of inception (DGRSDT, 2019a). These are distributed somewhat equally among the national territory, with the Centre hosting 478, the East 550, and the West 428 (2018 numbers) (DGRSDT, 2019a). In 2019, their regulations were updated by Ministerial decree,[37] stipulating that there must be at least four teams of at least three researchers each. There is an online directory for the latter, *DALILAB*,[38] searchable in French. In this framework, a recent quality assurance initiative can be noted, with the closing of 72 laboratories following an evaluation at the end of 2018 (University World News, 2018). Since 2000, a total

---

35   See the complete list: : http://atrst.dz/en/etablissements-de-recherche/
36   Structurally identical with the French system.
37   https://services.mesrs.dz/DEJA/fichiers_sommaire_des_textes/75%20bis%20fr.pdf, pp.6-10.
38   http://dalilab.dgrsdt.dz/site/

of 137 entities have been closed[39] (DGRSDT, 2019b). At the beginning of 2020, 66 new laboratories were established at a total of 44 universities, university centres, and écoles. The law also accounts for research teams, since 2013,[40] and – as recently as 2019 – thematic research networks[41]. As of the 1st quarter of 2020, 2,731 projects are listed in the online database of national research programmes in 34 thematic areas defined in 2008. Out of those, 312 were selected as having a socio-economic impact.

There are a total of 2,107 permanent researchers and 889 auxiliary research staff at national research institutes in the country, of which three-quarters are at *MESRS*-governed institutes. At the same time, they represented only 4% of the entire Algerian academic staff of approximately 55,000 in 2018 (DGRSDT, 2019a). Of these, 44% are female, and 56% male. Interestingly – arguably, contrary to many other national science settings – women make up more than 60% of the total in chemistry and natural sciences but still attain 40% in engineering and physics (DGRSDT, 2019b). In addition to doctoral candidate status, there are five ranks, in ascending order: *Maître Assistant (MA) A/B*, *Maître de Conférences (MC) A/B*, Professor. These ranks are applicable for both university-based as well as institute-based researchers[42].

Currently, the large proportion across all disciplines are doctoral candidates at 35%, followed by *MAA* with 27%, *MCA* with 12%, *MCB* with 11%, Professor at 10%, and – of little significance – *MAB* with 5% (DGRSDT, 2019b).[43] Therefore, it can be stated that the Algerian university staff is mainly

---

39   Information on the criteria for this decision or the affected researchers' positions after closing is unavailable

40   https://services.mesrs.dz/DEJA/fichiers_sommaire_des_textes/76%20FR%20A.PDF, pp.7–9.

41   https://services.mesrs.dz/DEJA/fichiers_sommaire_des_textes/71%20BIS%201%20fr.pdf, pp.15/16.

42   France features the same ranks, in use mainly at universities, although there are further functions in higher education institutions, too.

43   See also DRGRDT 2019a, p. 10, table 5 – partly calculated from absolute numbers and rounded off.

composed of those not having exercised research activities for long, as reflected in their lower scientific rank. The two categories of doctoral candidates and *MAA* have more than tripled since 2000, with the highest growth rate seen from 2001/2002 to 2011/2012. This fact also corresponds with the staff's age, with the highest proportion being 30–45 years old across all disciplines (DGRSDT, 2019b). It is noteworthy, too, that only 40% of those affiliated with research institutes are doctorate (PhD) holders, whereas the majority hold a master's degree. Of these personnel, 42% are active in the field of Engineering Sciences, with 11% and 9%, respectively, in the Arts and Humanities, and the Social Sciences (DGRSDT, 2019a). However, in terms of the total number of researchers as academic staff, roughly one-third each are engaged in either of these three fields (DGRSDT, 2019b).

Of the 13 national research centres under the tutelage of the Ministry, three are in humanities, and ten are in other disciplines – such as, notably, physics, including the most highly staffed centre, with 356 permanent researchers in 2018, the *Centre de Développement des* Énergies *Renouvelables (CDER).*[44] Two prominent non-science national research centres had existed before 2010, the *Centre de Recherche en* Économie *Appliquée pour le Développement (CREAD)*[45] and the *Centre de Recherche en Anthropologie Sociale et Culturelle (CRASC),*[46] established in 2006. The youngest national recent centre, on Islamic Sciences and Civilisation, dates from 2018 and has 37 staff members. Among the national institutes, too, is a multi-faceted research service, the Research Centre for Scientific and Technical Information (*CERIST*)[47] with 105 permanent researchers as of 2018, which hosts and administers, since 2012, the *Portail National de Signalement des Thèses (PNST),*[48] an online searchable directory of both

---

44   https://www.cder.dz/?lang=en
45   http://www.cread.dz/index.php/en/home-2/
46   https://www.crasc.dz/index.php/fr/
47   http://www.cerist.dz/index.php/en/
48   https://www.pnst.cerist.dz/

complete and on-going dissertations at the national level[49]. It also hosts the Algerian Scientific Journal Platform *(ASJP)*[50] for all national journals, and the centralised scientific journal and database access platform *(SNDL)*.[51] An update from March 2020 of the census of national scientific journals counts almost 700 nationally-published journals, in Arabic (491), French (166) and English (40) (DGRSDT, 2020). For international journals, it was customary in Algeria to publish an official categorisation, divided into categories A++, A, B, and C, but this has now been discontinued and replaced by a list of so-declared predatory journals/publishers of more than 1,000 each.

There are four so-called subsidiaries as spin-off institutes attached to national research centres in the fields of renewable energy, industrial technologies, physical-chemical analysis, and the centre for the development of advanced technologies, which deals with artificial intelligence. These are summarised under 'common research services',[52] which have a technical and technological orientation as platforms – including high-performance computing – and as for applied research, there has recently been a launch of incubators, two of which are already operational, two others under a feasibility study, and a further four are planned in the mid-term. Likewise, four Technology Transfer Centres, as well as Experimental Stations, are currently being implemented, conceptualised under the plan for development of scientific research and technological development 2008–2012. Not least, there are 'Research and Development Centres',[53] which are hosted at the biggest (parastatal) industries, such as SONATRACH for fossil fuels exploitations, CEVITAL

---

49   France has parallel structures: i.e. CNRS Institutes, the
       Unité Régionale de Formation à l'Information Scientifique
       et Technique (URFIST)/ thesis.fr
50   https://www.asjp.cerist.dz/
51   http://www.cerist.dz/index.php/en/portails-2/809-sndl
52   See section on the DRGSDT website, http://www.dgrsdt.dz/
       v1/index.php?fc=Plt_Tech
53   See subsection of research structures on the DGRSDT
       website: http://www.dgrsdt.dz/v1/index.php?fc=St_RSDT

for food processing, the HASNAOUI Group in construction and agriculture, and the National Enterprise of Electronic Industries/Electrical Goods. To complement the knowledge transfer entities, there also exist so-called *clubs scientifiques*, which are student initiatives on university campuses[54].

The Algerian national university commission is also in charge of the evaluation and promotion of *enseignant-chercheurs*, so-called lecturer-researchers in professorial capacities at universities.[55] Established in 1994, it was complemented by the national commission of researcher evaluation in 2009.[56] After its creation in 2004, the functioning of the national commission of habilitation[57] was modified in 2015, together with an update of the national commission for doctoral-level studies (*troisième cycle*) in 2019[58] after establishment in 2007. Since 2013, there has been a Deans' conference,[59] according to discipline. Furthermore, there is the national scientific commission for validation of scientific journals, existing since 2014,[60] with the provision for former 'C category' national journals from 2018, updated in 2019.[61] The commission for the implementation of a quality assurance system (*CIAQES*)[62] dates from 2010. From 2019, a commission

---

54   See Chapter VI: Vie étudiante et insertion professionnelle, Section IV, Les clubs scientifiques au sein des établissements d'enseignement supérieur https://www. mesrs.dz/fr/chapitre6

55   https://services.mesrs.dz/DEJA/fichiers_sommaire_des_textes/24%20FR.PDF

56   https://services.mesrs.dz/DEJA/fichiers_sommaire_des_textes/25%20AR.PDF (Arabic)

57   https://services.mesrs.dz/DEJA/fichiers_sommaire_des_textes/19%20bis%20fr.pdf

58   https://services.mesrs.dz/DEJA/fichiers_sommaire_des_textes/26%20FR.pdf

59   https://services.mesrs.dz/DEJA/fichiers_sommaire_des_textes/26%20B%20FR.PDF

60   https://services.mesrs.dz/DEJA/fichiers_sommaire_des_textes/26%20A%202%20FR.pdf

61   https://services.mesrs.dz/DEJA/fichiers_sommaire_des_textes/26%20F%2B.pdf (Arabic)

62   http://www.ciaqes-mesrs.dz/

for the selection of candidates for leadership positions of higher education institutions has been operational.[63]

With the two *DGRSDT* reports serving as a blueprint for a national research strategy and sectoral research strategy in the years to come, both outline the main challenges as follows: firstly, there is the absence of a special legal status for permanent researchers, and, secondly, conditions in general are not favourable for staff at research institutes as compared to academic staff – *enseignants-chercheurs* – at universities (DGRSDT, 2019a).

As for scientific production, in 2023, there were 116123 publications and 1257462 citations, corresponding to approximately 6,67% of the African total, 5,81 % of the Arab countries', and 0,27% of the worldwide output. Out of those, just under 50% were with international co-authorship, and around 40 % open access. As of the first quarter of 2024, as per SCOPUS data, Algerian occupies the 6th rank in African classification, after South Africa, Egypt, Nigeria and Tunisia, Morocco – and before Ethiopia, Kenya and Ghana in the Top 10 – and ranks 60th worldwide, based on a bibliometric analysis with data from the open-access Scimago Journal and Country Rank Portal'.[64] After its peak in 2008, since 2018, a decline in ranking position can be observed. In 2018 still, when aggregated per discipline, Algeria ranks among the top three in Africa in physics, chemistry, material sciences, engineering and mathematics; as opposed to economics/finance (11th) and psychology (19th) and, on a worldwide scale, Algeria's best position is again in material sciences (42), engineering (44) and mathematics (45), with a total of nine disciplines out of 27 in the top 50. Towards the lower end, once more, there are social sciences (71), arts and humanities (80), and psychology (113) (DGRSDT, 2019c). The citation rate per document, as an indicator of the national scientific production, is relatively low in the arts and humanities, and social sciences, at only one-

63   https://services.mesrs.dz/DEJA/fichiers_sommaire_des_ textes/26D++FR.pdf
64   https://www.scimagojr.com

third of the national average, which is likely due to default Arabic-language publications in these fields as well as lower standards for journal reputation compared with natural sciences, according to the authors of the study (DGRSDT, 2019c). While there seems to be no correlation with increased research funding, a correlation between the increase in researchers and improved scientific productivity can be observed (DGRSDT, 2019c).

3.3 Phases of National and International Orientation

It is a risky task for any educational leader to attempt to transform a system as vast as the university in such a short time without a trial or pilot study. The Algerian university system of higher education does manifest certain common trends and phenomena that are leading it to a greater resemblance to the Maghrib nations as a whole (Daghbouche, 2011, p. 469).

The national policies of a newly independent Algeria, which naturally influenced its university and emerging higher education system, were set at the Congress of Tripoli in 1962, followed by the Constitution in 1963 and the Charter of Algiers 1964. Three main lines of the ensuing policy were the emphasis on science, the acknowledgement of the values of Arab–Islamic civilisation, and loyalty towards socialism (Mahiou, 2015, p. 9). The first indication of reform of the colonial higher education system was the establishment of the commission of higher education reform in the Ministry for National Education in 1967. In 1969, a national commission of educational reform was established.

Then-President Houari Boumediene (1965–1978) stated in one of his speeches on Arabisation, within the framework of the commission, that '*la langue arabe est la langue de la sidérurgie et de l'acier*'[65] (Mahiou, 2013, p. 301),

---

65   'The Arabic language is the language of steel and the steel industry.'

thus making Arabisation another priority as a means of national development, as was the policy of the *FLN* cultural commission, which sought 'indépendance linguistique' after political independence from France (Mahiou, 2015, p. 11). Then-Minister and president of the commission, Ahmed Taleb, took over to define the four pillars of higher education reform: Algerianisation of academic staff, Arabisation of instruction in a 'de facto' bilingual environment, the democratisation of higher education in line with other levels of national education, and scientific modernisation (Mahiou, 2015, p. 10).

After a government re-shuffle and a partition of the former Ministry for National Education into two separate Ministries of Higher Education and Basic Education in 1971, the first reform of higher education was designed by European, the former Soviet Union and American educational consultancies, which, although it may seem paradoxical for the socialist regime of the time, had put the university on an economy-oriented, developmental, and even liberal, as well as global, pathway (Bellil, 1985; Mammeri, 1989; Guerid, 2007). Nevertheless, the Ministry explicitly drew on experience from fellow socialist countries such as the then Soviet Union, in planning higher education development (Daghbouche, 1982, p. 47), although elected Deans of the University of Algiers as delegation members participated in month-long hospitation visits to the United States and the former Yugoslavia. Subsequently, experts from around the world, such as Canadians, French, Chileans, Brazilians, Yugoslavians, and Egyptians are reported to have taken part in the evaluation of proposals put forward by committees dedicated to each discipline (Mahiou, 2015, p. 15).

The formula employed, seen as an adequate measure, was '*une formation maximale au moindre coût*'[66] and it entailed removing the rest of the universities' autonomy (Ghalamallah, 2006, p. 35). The door was thus open for all kinds of political and ideological instrumentalisation to prevail at the university

---

66   'a maximum of training at the lowest cost.'

(Ghalamallah, 2006, p. 36). Following three national seminars on 'Formation et développement' in 1968, 1970 and 1971, tertiary education was 'assimilated' in the sense of re-organised to resemble a factory, with the students as workers towards the goals of development and modernisation (Guerid, 2007). From this background, Institutes of Technology were founded, as well as Écoles *polytechniques*, which also determined the hierarchy of disciplines, i.e., experimental and engineering sciences at the top of the hierarchy, for technical, practice-oriented training, and training of a more vocational nature lower down the hierarchy.

Arabisation itself was implemented in several phases. Firstly, in the 1960s, it only applied to history and philosophy; secondly, in the 1970s, law, social sciences and sciences were taught bilingually, in Arabic and French in parallel. Thirdly, in the 1980s, social sciences were entirely Arabised, and fourthly, from the 1990s, the division of social sciences and humanities into Arabic, and experimental sciences in French, respectively, was implemented. (Guerid, 2010). Accordingly, over two decades from 1970 to 1990, programmatic teaching was prescribed to mitigate drawbacks resulting from instructors' weak pedagogic and subject competences, with no systematic evaluation that would have led to measures such as closing poorly-performing public education institutions. There was even a tendency among supervisors to dogmatise national education policy by encouraging or favouring those thesis subjects treating related pedagogical, didactical or organisational aspects (Haddab, 2014, p. 249). French-taught science and engineering academic programmes received the first cohort of Arabic-educated baccalaureate holders in 1989. In contrast, the Arabisation reform was generalised from 1990, leading to the implementation of Arabic as the language of instruction for scientific disciplines, except medicine. Training on the use of Arabic was conducted through regional conferences of university lecturers during the period of Djilali Liabes, a humanities professor and Minister from 1991 until his assassination in 1993.

In 1980, Minister Mustapha Haddab's predecessor in office, from 1966 to 1971, and later UNESCO Director, Mourad Benachenhou, underlined the revolutionary character of the Algerian university: '*Dans les sociétés révolutionnaires, lancées dans la remise en cause de l'ordre social et l'avènement d'un monde plus juste, l'université constituera une institution privilégiée dans la Révolution. Et c'est justement le cas dans notre pays*'[67] (Benachenhou, 1980). Further, he describes the institution's education mission as training technically competent civil servants, imbued with the Algerian personality, aware of national realities and active in the process of a socialist development (Benachenhou, 1980). Daghbouche, too, affirms this view by underlining the pragmatic and applied feature of the late 1970s Algerian university: '(...) a university is itself a product of society and the above conception of autonomy is an abstraction far from the way the real world works' (Daghbouche, 1982, p. 11). She sums up its objective as follows: (...) higher education is regarded by government as a means of furthering development, and by individuals as a means of improving their personal economic prospects' (Daghbouche, 1982, p. 15) as well as, through learning how to learn, both independently and in Arabic, the '(...) base for real change in the life style of the country' (Daghbouche, 1982, p. 27).

As one of the most prominent representatives of the contemporary diaspora, Aïssa Kadri exhibits this claim in his article 'From the colonial to the national university. Instrumentalisation and "ideologization" of the institution' (in French). He stipulates that, '*Il n'est pas autrement extrêmement hardi, (...) de déceler dans les fonctions assumées par le système d'enseignement colonial et le système de l'enseignement national une homologie quasi parfaite*'[68] (Kadri, 1991), p.153). For him, the Algerian university is characterised

---

67   'In revolutionary societies, launched into the questioning of the social order and the advent of a more just world, the university will be a privileged institution in the Revolution. And this is precisely the case in our country.'

68   'It is not unduly daring (...) to detect, in the functions assumed by the colonial educational system and the system of national education, an almost perfect homology.'

by '(...) *une continuité de fond et des fonctions: un enseignement fortement idéologisé, instrumentalisé, s'inscrivant dans un procès de contrôle politique de l'institution et de la production des élites*'[69] (Kadri, 1991). Hence, the definition of the university institution is its integration in the larger political project with a national outlook (Kadri, 1991).

In line with this argument, but more general and thus fluid, the Algerian university is portrayed as an agent of economic and social development (Djeflat, 1990, p. 36). As opposed to earlier or parallel prevailing theoretical reflections, Djeflat argues from a quantitative empirical basis. First and foremost, the university is to produce graduates for the productive sector, and among its contributions to social development, the accessibility to, and, improvement of, women's education is significant (Djeflat, 1990, pp. 48–49). Indeed, there was a long-term social status ascendency aspect during the first decades after independence, characterised as '*l'efficacité sociologique du système* éducatif'[70] (Haddab, 2014, p. 241) of the Algerian higher education system.

Since 2004, however, a gradual shift in policy towards internationalisation can be observed in the adoption of the Bologna Process, applied to selected pilot universities at first, as has been detailed above, based on decrees[71] in 2008, first for bachelor and secondly for master's courses, in effect from 2007/2008 and 2008/2009, respectively, followed by a gradual nation-wide roll-out. The official permit to operate private higher education institutions opens doors for foreign operators, too. Academic excellence has also been highlighted recently, as can be seen from the new Minister's initiative to establish centres focusing on, for example, artificial

---

69   '(...) a continuity of substance and functions: a strongly ideologised, instrumentalised teaching, part of a process of political control of the institution and the production of the elite.'
70   'The sociological effectiveness of the education system.'
71   In particular, law 08-06 (pp.33-37) and decrees 06-265, 09-03, 08-130, 10-231. Cf. https://www.mesrs.dz/ habilitations-de-formations-lmd. See also Baddari and Herzallah (2014)

intelligence, sustainable development, medical sciences, and economics from the beginning of 2020 (MESRS, 2020c).

Alignment to international standards of quality assurance has recently been placed on the agenda with the creation of a national council on ethics and deontology, with the mission of developing mandatory courses as well as anti-plagiarism measures, among others (MESRS, 2020b). In February 2020, the then-Minister reiterated these plans through the installation of ethics councils, to be implemented at university level, too (Bensouiah, 2020d). The new government has also initiated outreach activities involving the Algerian diaspora (Bensouiah, 2020c). In mid-2019, the interim government, while awaiting elections after Abdelaziz Bouteflika's resignation in April 2019, announced plans to promote English as well as Arabic as languages of instruction in Algerian higher education, and to reduce the presence of French. The former Minister, in the first half of 2020, did not actively work towards implementation of this language policy, and was instead focusing on the quality of education, regardless of the language used (Bensouiah, 2020a).

Furthermore, there has recently been an announcement of the prospect of a common Arab university classification spearheaded by Egypt (Bensouiah, 2019b). There are two bi-national cooperation agreements, namely, with the Republic of Iran, ratified by presidential decree in 2017, and, more recently, with the United States of America, since the beginning of 2019 (MESRS, 2020a). There have been multi-lateral agreements with Tunisia, Morocco, Mauritania since 2010, as well as the 'Regional Convention on the Recognition of Studies, Certificates, Diplomas, Degrees and Other Certificates of Higher Education in African States' since 1981, coming into effect in 1988. The recognition of degrees obtained abroad has also been updated and facilitated after its first provision in 1971, complemented by decrees in 2013 and 2015, and by ministerial decree in 2018.[72] Of these requests, 70% concern

---

72   See Chapter III, Section II, Les documents demandés pour
       le dossier d'obtention d'équivalence des diplômes et titres

the recognition of French diplomas in Algeria (Mediterranean Network of National Information Centres on the Recognition of Qualifications [MERIC-Net], 2019).

In terms of research support, Algeria is also involved in the European Commission's 'Horizon 2020' as well as European Cooperation in Science and Technology (COST) programmes.[73] Algeria had participated in the TEMPUS programme for more than a decade (2002–2014), with more than fifty partnership projects including updating curricula, implementing quality assurance in academic activities, and developing relations with socio-economic partners, employers and industries. The *Renforcement de l'assurance qualité interne dans les universités de la Méditerranée (AQI-UMED)*[74] project produced an internal quality assurance standard for Mediterranean universities involving European, Moroccan, Tunisian and Algerian universities in 2010–2013. This project has since become the *Référentiel National d'Assurance Qualité de l'Enseignement Supérieur (RNAQES)*. Several Algerian students were involved in 15 Erasmus Mundus mobility projects from 2007 to 2014 (Benstaali, 2019). Algeria currently participates in the EU's Erasmus + programme[75] and, in early 2020, the third 'Algerian-Spanish Pre-Call' (ALGESIP)[76] was also announced. Regarding research, the focus is internationalisation according to different indicators in the coming years until 2025, as outlined in the provisional strategy 'Horizon 2025' (DGRSDT, 2019a).

Overall, the structure of the Algerian higher education and research system, despite reforms entailing reorganisation and Arabisation, remains similar or even equivalent to France in its institutions, organograms, governance, and selection processes. In this sense, there are still *legs colonial* (Bayard & Bertrand, 2006), or post-colonial elements that are to

---

universitaires étrangers https://www.mesrs.dz/fr/chapitre3
73   http://www.h2020.dz/#programme
74   http://www.agence-erasmus.fr/docs/2161_livret-aqiumed.pdf (in French)
75   http://erasmusplus.dz/index.php/fr/accueil/
76   http://www.dgrsdt.dz/v1/index.php?fc=Appels_A&id=61

be dealt with and tackled. Although Algeria has sought to overcome these – first by policies strengthening both so-called Algerianisation and nationalisation, and, more recently, by adopting policies in favour of internationalisation – parallel structures continue to affect Algerian education. Their influence results in ambivalences on various levels, which are discussed in the next section.

4. Ambivalences through Personal Oscillations

Algerian academics are confronted with system ambivalences between the national and the international, as has become apparent in contradictory university functions related to ideology and the particular post-colonial situation of the Algerian university. This situation leads to a personal oscillation, or uncertainty, regarding engaging in research, i.e., the decision to do so or refrain from it. The specific ambivalences causing these oscillations are, on the one hand, policy-induced and system-based, and on the other hand, derived from the transformation element of internationalisation exposure and associated challenges in reform, as well as the absence of a strategy to serve as orientation for personal action.

4.1 National: Policy-Induced and System-based

Democratisation versus Massification

To begin with, there is an ambivalence in policy, since, on the one hand, by continuing to add new institutions to the system, all universities within the country are considered equal in principle, as their mission is to grant access to higher education to the entirety of the Algerian high-school leavers. This perspective is connected with exclusively public funding, and is accepted as common knowledge as encapsulated in the following: '(…) besides, we don't have a university for the elites here, we don't have it; we don't have an elite university. Access to university is open, that's it (…)' (15_m_Arts_Humanities_ Social Sciences_administrative function_faculty).

On the other hand, institutions themselves may be attributed elitist status by the governing body; '(…) It is the Ministry which chose its pilot universities (…)', yet those in charge at the institutional level feel obliged to create a balance for the benefit of the whole system by practising knowledge transfer; '(...) but what is good, everyone should be aware of this, it's sharing and good practice' (7_m_Arts_Humanities_Social Sciences_executive function_central unit). This is an expression of their state of oscillation.

At the same time, competitive advantages of institutions are emphasised by their executive representatives, which appear in the form of pioneering developments, e.g., evaluation, as in the following case: 'So, I told you, this self-assessment process has started in Algeria since 2016. There was a national benchmark to develop this self-assessment (...)' (6_m_Arts_Humanities_Social Sciences_executive function_central_unit) or, indeed, refer to the socio-economic conditions: '(...) Imagine, the Rector, once, he said: "Hold on, do you know where Adrar is? It's in the deep South. If the people of this Wilaya send their daughter here, it's because they trust us." You see what I mean. So, there is the environment, there is also the environment!' (9_f_STEM_executive function_research unit).

Nevertheless, the issue of massification has exposed the qualitative versus the quantitative conflict; '(...) you have number versus quality, that means, can we provide quality training for such a large number (...)?' (14_m_STEM_administrative function_central unit). Hence, there is an ambivalent situation, since both education for all and quality cannot be guaranteed: 'Lack of knowledge. They don't have the pre-requirements. More so, massification has brought about people that, who do not have capacities, but we make them ascend' (10_m_Arts_Humanities_Social Sciences_executive function_research unit). Hence, Algerian academics oscillate between their attributed function and their observations as members of society.

It is acknowledged that there is an ambivalence with the quantification; 'Difficult to choose (laughs), because it mixes. At times, it is massification, at times democratisation, but deciding between the two is difficult. *Humm. It goes together.* That goes together. We can't separate the two' (6_m_Arts_

Humanities_Social Sciences_executive function_central unit). These two perspectives are due to system factors – politically-induced facilitation of access rooted in historic inequalities – versus individuals' opinions, connected to their status and role. It is first pointed out that this development, although recent, has impacted all the more intensely:

> So, first of all, Algeria went from the 80s to the 2000s through a process of massification of education. That means, us, in our time, we still had quality education because the number was limited. Yes. And so, we had a lecturer-student relation that was up to the norm. Algeria made a choice, which is to allow everyone to go to university. So it's a massification of higher education; yes …which means that today, we have; we have practically multiplied the number of students in all fields by three, by four, even by five sometimes (...) (3_f_STEM).

Given their apparent non-political role as academics; '(Laughs) I am not to comment on the role of the Ministry, but …' (6_m_Arts_Humanities_Social Sciences_executive function_central unit), policy decisions and mode of governance may not be questioned. Consequently, Algerian academics may find themselves in a position of oscillation in this system of what they perceive as massification in the context of political democratisation of the higher education system. They may hint at respective governance structures, such as; 'Democratisation? I don't know. I would say decentralisation, much more so' (4_5_f_Arts_Humanities_ Social Sciences_1_administrative function_central unit). Indeed, the notion of democratisation may also be explicitly and outspokenly rejected, as in the following: '(...) I'm not very comfortable with the term "democratisation", because, really, really, really, we are not in a democratic regime, to talk about, "democracy", and "democratisation" (...)' (16_m_Arts_ Humanities_Social Sciences). The latter opinion is voiced repeatedly:

Of course, it will not work. It is obvious that it will not work. As a system, that's it, as a system. This whole system, it's a populist system, populist, under the pretext and under the guise of democratisation of education; that's why I reacted just before when you said 'democratisation'. It's not true. It's not democratisation; it's total populism. We give all of them higher degrees, but in fact, we do not have an overview of the professional integration of all these graduates. And when we do not have an overview of economic integration, it means we are also selling off the economic sector (3_f_STEM).

Here, as another aspect to the debate, the criticism mentioned is aimed at the lack of other, and varied, tertiary education options, including vocational, which are not addressed in an ideology-loaded official discourse of access, and postgraduate and research training:

So why, on the pretext that we have to democratise then we have to allow everyone to hope to be a doctor and a professor, when they are people who have skills in other fields. Yes. So for me, 'democratisation of education', it is a term which is completely empty of meaning. Okay, yes. It does mean absolutely nothing for me. Because, if not, we would oppose it to the confiscation of education and teaching. But we don't confiscate; it's not because we don't want massification that we confiscate knowledge and training. But we distribute it more consistently and in a much more ideal manner (3_f_STEM).

While some mention the negative aspects of having a university in each *Wilaya* – with cultural and personal development hampered by not broadening horizons, as opposed to post-independence times of only one university and two centres as annexes country-wide – '(…), I cannot say the opposite. There was an advantage, it is that of giving, even just a certain level, even if it is low, but a level of education which allowed him to see how the others lived' (10_m_Arts_ Humanities_Social Sciences_executive function_research unit), others emphasise the lack of distinctiveness of a single higher education institution from a nation-building point of view; 'One, it would have strengthened national unity. We are a country. A young nation, it would have allowed mingling of students and staff from all regions, and it would have allowed a concentration of qualifications, too' (1_m_Arts_ Humanities_Social Sciences_research).

From an academic perspective, with regards to research, a massification of institutions is also problematic, as '(...) Universities cannot flourish when they are numerous and geographically located in the same region (...)' (7_m_Arts_ Humanities_Social Sciences_executive function_central unit), so they lose, cannot retain, or never develop their status as centres of excellence. Not least, executives themselves are affected by the massified system at their institutions, and are called upon to undertake a major task, as in this case:

> (...) But these little things of administrative constraints, it has always existed, and they will always exist, maybe less and less, but they will exist — the administrative slowness. Now, we are fixing everything. Students were taking a long time to have their diplomas. Now, they have them very quickly. We have a Rector who signs ten thousand diplomas in one week (...) (7_m_Arts_Humanities_Social Sciences_ executive function_central unit).

Individually, there is an ambivalent situation for Algerian lecturers because of the inflation of academic degrees, with frustration regarding the usefulness of one's work:

> (...) Because, as I told you just before, it is not the diploma that gives us the right to teach (laughs). And what is currently being done, it's not... Even less if everyone has the diploma. Yes, yes, that's it, that means even more. It's heartbreaking to find people who only think about the diploma. Because with the diploma, one can access. But a diploma is not everything. Yes, no, especially since there is inflation in general. Yes, it can no longer continue (10_m_

Arts_Humanities_Social Sciences_executive function_ research unit).

Further, circumstances of higher education system expansion and student number increases have a detrimental effect on teaching, which becomes obvious first in the technical disciplines; '(...) That means, at master 1 level, they are taken care of by the research laboratory, and so, you must imagine the situation. If you have the first year of master with about twenty students, and the second year of master with twenty students, forty students in a laboratory, it's a bit annoying, for practical work especially (...)' (13_m_STEM_administrative function_faculty). In addition, even medical studies, generally considered elitist and hence restricted, have become subject to massification:

> (...) Massification, there was an explosion in the number of students. I had students; before, I give you an example, in 93, we sometimes had up to 100 (*STEM discipline*) students. 93. We are in 2018; we have up to 500 students in the same lecture theatre. That, it's a massification, indeed, because we are victim of the number of students who register. We have no choice (...) (8_f_STEM).

This statement shows the disapproval of the professor with the current policy, yet also exposes their lack of decision-making power.

The social sciences and humanities, too, are affected by the status quo of a context-dependent and coerced lack of quality assurance non-conducive to academia and its training; '(...) It may be shocking what I tell you, but we end up with legions of students and with little requirements on what they have to produce. *That's it*. That is, it's not normal, it's not normal I mean, it is ... (...)' (1_m_Arts_Humanities_ Social Sciences_research). This state of affairs is even more pronounced at the postgraduate level; '(...) One cannot, it is... to seriously attend to 120 master students (...)' (Paragraph 62), which then leads to the following situation of lecturers being overwhelmed and students' lack of attention:

(...) let's put it this way. There are too many students now, and the infrastructure is not enough to get everybody, so you end up having a lot of students in one room and so you can't communicate with everybody. So, people ... you suffer, and the students suffer even more (2_m_STEM_research).

System-based Factors

There are factors that are system-inherent and thus governance-based. To begin with, there is the challenge of inadequate foreign language skills, which is based on school-level policy; '(...) I have to tell you one of the problems we have, also we have the children are getting education, Arabic education, after they get to do university starting French (laughs) this is why you need one year more, one more year I am sorry' (2_m_STEM_research) and this places academics in a situation of personal oscillation. This ambivalence extends to both teaching as part of their duties,

> (...) it's neither Arabic nor French. People should apply a system. These days, our students know neither Arabic nor French. That's a big problem. Yes. And when you hear them, speak at the level of institutions, or at TV, people cannot string a sentence in the same language: two words in Arabic, two words in French, two words in English. It has become gibberish; it is no longer; it is no longer a real language. That's why it's a problem. But I think it will fade in a few years (10_m_Arts_Humanities_Social Sciences_ executive function_research unit).

and to research, taking into account required language competences: '(...) it's, for a researcher, it's doing the work halfway. We can't; we can't say that we did monolingual research. It is not possible. Because me, I think in one way, another person can think in another way, I need to know his ideas' (10_m_Arts_Humanities_Social Sciences_executive function_research unit).

Importantly, there are insufficient university administration staff, which forces Algerian academics to take on extra-curricular projects, apart from teaching and engaging in research:

> (...) when we take a European university the size of the university (institution), all these structures, (name), incubator, etc., it's at least 60 people full-time. It's at least, minimum, 60 people full-time. And management, not research, not teaching. They don't teach; they don't do research. They manage this structure. That's the problem (14_m_STEM_administrative function_central unit).

As the above statement shows, this gap becomes apparent only when compared to institutions abroad, although every member of the Algerian academia is arguably in this situation; 'But it's true, it is true that each structure needs an organogram. It is clear. If not, a lecturer-researcher will be overwhelmed. One needs administrative support' (14_m_STEM_administrative function_central unit). Administrative processes, in general, are perceived as too bureaucratic and lengthy, which then hamper research, as is openly admitted in the following: '(...) There are ..., sometimes there are administrative procedures, which may interfere. It is true that they are made to order, to organise, but it's not always the case. Sometimes, in trying to apply the regulations to the letter, we handicap a lot of the, the, the ... *Activities* ... Of research activities (...)' (6_m_Arts_ Humanities_Social Sciences_executive function_central unit).

Furthermore, the lack of financial incentive to engage in research is highlighted, too, as a system-based factor derived from a largely non-existent evaluation and assessment;

> (...) If one positively assesses a researcher, one will also be able to support, especially financially, etc. for research projects abroad or, or even here at home, projects that require, for example, more funding or at least more resources. But there is no evaluation, so there is no requirement of results. And that, if it were to be at the international standard, to return to the question on international standards there, yes, it is necessary, it must

be applied, that is to say, that: an evaluation is a follow-up (...) (1_m_Arts_Humanities_Social Sciences_research).

This situation leads to frustration as a result of the personal oscillation between going the extra mile in engaging in research, or letting things go by refraining from it.

The absence of budget autonomy proves problematic as well: '*For this, it would be necessary... well, to have one's own budget? Which is presently not the case.* Yes, it's logical. Already, to have the budget, you have to prove that there are results. And step-by-step, as there are results, there is budget. It's a vicious circle' (8_9_f_STEM_1_executive function_research unit).

In this context, the system foresees no job recruitment post-doctorate either, a decision that is not taken by the head of the research unit, which leads to the loss of talent:

The doctoral student, once he finishes, he finds a position elsewhere, he leaves. If he can't find a job, he has no rights in the lab. He can come for research, but he can't have anything, for example. That is not good either. Because otherwise, it would help keep people here, that's it. There is a law, a law which has been passed. It must be ... because when we have a law, we have the law and the ..., the application (8_9_f_STEM_1_executive function_ research unit).

Hence, there is neither budgetary nor human resources decision-making autonomy, which greatly restricts research activities, and leaves academics to oscillate between their mission and the reality of the system they operate in.

On a meso level, institutional autonomy, too, would be needed to develop and succeed with regards to research outcomes:

(...) I think they should give more liberty or more freedom to the rectors of the universities. Mm-hmm. Maybe so they should some guidelines but then let them work, I think that

> would be the best way. Because when you ... everything is centralised the way to do it in Algeria whereas you have the Ministry and the way it is (unclear 00:44:35-7) are two different things, two different philosophy. Most of the time the people in Algeria don't feel what the local needs are and I think we should give them some freedom. So, it is I would say more like more regulatory system then somebody who gets involve into details, to me that's the way it should be (2_m_STEM_research).

The criticism put forward here is that the governing body does not take the individual situation on the ground into account, and, consequently, does not act in a needs-based way, whereas leadership of a university could very well do the appropriate thing for their institution, if given the legal avenues to do so. Once more, those in an executive position oscillate between what is centrally decided or prescribed, and what they assess as an institutional plan.

Lastly, at the macro level, the absence of a wider Algerian societal development plan, where the university would play an intermediary role, has been identified. This leaves academics without a clear plan in assuming their teaching function: 'We don't have a societal plan. If you want to know, we don't have it. Even if they say that our objective is to train, to train to ensure the tomorrow. But train what? (...)' (10_m_Arts_ Humanities_Social Sciences_executive function_research unit). Hence, the personal oscillation of lecturer and society member is reflected. This lack of strategy, and hence the orientation, becomes even more apparent in the following:

> (...) 'You know well that you have taught us that a programme can only be built on a societal project. Then, you ask us to do a programme without having the project of society'. In 97, they did not answer us, in 98, they did not answer us, and that at the level of the Ministry. In 99, I said with the one who was with me, 'I swear that we will not leave here without them telling us what the project of society is'. The answer was unacceptable: 'We expect it from you'. That means that nothing was done, and so

far, we have no societal project. How will Algeria live? (...) (10_m_Arts_Humanities_Social   Sciences_executive function_research unit).

4.2   International: Transformation and Challenges

Challenges in Internationalisation Exposure

Stakeholders in Algerian academia, including lecturer-researchers, suffer from one-sided or disadvantageous cooperation, examples of which are detailed in the following. Algerian-conferred degrees are not recognised abroad by default, resulting in graduates having to repeat at least six months: '(...) there is always a year or six months of refresher' (4_5_f_Arts_Humanities_Social Sciences_1_administrative function_central unit). This state of affairs applies to STEM subjects all the more:

> (...) We should do statistics. I know that in our scientific and technical disciplines, they make up a very, very large part. After all, do they have the means for it? How are they perceived and received elsewhere? That is yet another story. Because being weak; these days, equivalences are more and more difficult to give (3_f_STEM).

Administrative difficulties continue to persist, hampering individual progress: 'Well, abroad, I ... What did I see? No, I went to France several times; I went to Turkey, too, and I visited (*public educational institution outside of higher education*). So it was not, I did not have access (...) I went to Turkey, but I did not have the opportunity to have the cooperation agreement and the authorisations to access the university; it was a little difficult (...)' (4_5_f_Arts_Humanities_Social Sciences_1_administrative function_central unit) Another reason is ill-designed exchange programmes, where necessary language requirements cannot be met, as the following case shows:

We made an agreement with them so that we could have distance education. But it will only be in English. Yes, because they master neither French nor Arabic. So, we can't. Well, a few, anyway. No, but it is, above all; first of all, people who can be at university must, normally, it is the three languages that they must be...; but here, it is two languages, if need be, two languages, one, they know it well, the other, more difficult. But I see that people are going towards English (...) (10_m_Arts_Humanities_ Social Sciences_executive function_research unit).

Financial difficulties in Algerian aggravate the situation, driving emigration for economic reasons:

(...) At the moment, in conjuncture of the fall in the price of barrels; the reduction of the state income, so, exhaustion of the financial state reserves, so, it's a more delicate conjuncture. Automatically, people flee from their country; one thinks of escaping the country. I apologise for the term. So, we must review this situation, and give hope to these youth who want to go to France or elsewhere. It's not only to France. There are students all over the world: United States, Japan, Germany (...) (15_m_Arts_Humanities_ Social Sciences_administrative function_faculty).

Nevertheless, France continues to be a reference and is the preferred destination for graduates and postgraduates:

(...) well, now the internationalisation, it is done, as you said earlier, it is done in one direction only. It is especially the Algerian students, and the best, trained here, until the bachelor, up to the master, who are leaving, you see? To enter international circuits. But the opposite direction is not done; the opposite is not done. I take, for example, there are a lot of students here, with the master. They will try their luck, they will try their luck, principally in France (...) (16_m_Arts_Humanities_Social Sciences).

This status quo may have arisen through a French policy of promoting and providing scholarships: 'Because she was the best in class, among the best in class, so she received a scholarship, a French scholarship; not an Algerian scholarship. Her supervisor is an Algerian' (11_f_STEM). Accordingly, emigration for educational purposes, especially to France, may be commonly justified as follows: '(…) students, in particular, must continue their studies, because for them, continuing studies in France, it's the future, it is access to their futures. So, there is no need to fight; to hold back these youth' (15_m_ Arts_Humanities_Social Sciences_administrative function_ faculty).

Further system-induced factors are a need to change the working culture; '(…) So, but more important for me, is this: one, that they get used to working all the time, all the time, all the time. It is not always obvious for the Mediterraneans' (9_f_STEM_executive function_research unit). There is a discrepancy between work habits at home and abroad; 'I think you have to be authoritarian. I think you have to be authoritarian, no, at first, be authoritarian, get people used to it, and after a while, it will become a normal habit. When they are abroad, they are in the lab; we are sometimes in the lab from 7am until 10, 9pm' (8_9_f_STEM_1_executive function_research unit).

Absence of Internationalisation Strategy

The Ministry as the responsible central governing body is in charge of Algerian higher education internationalisation, which is put forward as common knowledge by individual Algerian academics: '*Okay. Those who decide on that is it…?* It is the Ministry, yes. It's the cooperation service. *So, it's very centralised? The governance?* Yes, yes, quite, rather' (4_5_f_Arts_Humanities_Social Sciences_1_ administrative function_central unit). However, the status quo of Algerian higher education, from an individual perspective, is characterised by the absence of a strategy of internationalisation as is shown by the following statements: 'And the current strategy is entering the world' (9_f_STEM_ executive function_research unit); 'And there are the Arab countries, it's normal, so there are a lot of lecturers going to Arab countries, so it's normal' (6_m_Arts_Humanities_ Social Sciences_executive function_central unit); '(...) There is always, there are relations with the United States, there are relations with the countries of Eastern Europe' (...) ; (...) 'There are also now countries that give scholarships (...)' (6_m_ Arts_Humanities_Social Sciences_excutive function_central unit).

Therefore, various countries or regions are mentioned, without any focus on area, language, ideology, or (geo)political considerations. Notwithstanding, national institutional profiling may occur through its internationalisation degree. The latter serves as a distinct identity. However, there is a general and apparent discrepancy between international ranking and national status, as is shown in the following:

> Yes, for publications, so, each year there is the ranking, and so the university (institution), the ranking has been improved, from the start of these rankings until the present. We were at 4000 and something; we are at 2000 and something; we still won 2000 places. We are still far, but still, we gained 2000 places. By national ranking, this is (institution specificity) (...) (13_m_STEM_administrative function_faculty).

It is up to the institution to position themselves as active in the internationalisation development; '(...) The internationalisation side, cooperation side, it differs between university and others. There are universities that are really advanced, there are others that are not, which start, and there are also universities which have relations, but it is on a personal basis' (6_m_Arts_Humanities_Social Sciences_ executive function_central unit).

However, these individual cases do not make up for the lack of a needs analysis, which is said not to have taken place before the Bologna reform was introduced:

> You were talking earlier about LMD, etc.; well, I have the impression that it was done without a deep reflection on: does it correspond to the local situation? That's it; I do not think that this reflection was made, we have, we applied it like that, we thought that there is an international standard and that it should be applied without reflection; that's it; I have this impression; hm; well we have had others, we have other concerns in cooperation (1_m_Arts_Humanities_ Social Sciences_research).

Correspondingly, other national policy decisions, as internationalisation adaptation measures, have been top-down only; 'So, the Ministry saw that it was necessary to standardise, and there was standardisation, which started from the year 2017' (6_m_Arts_Humanities_Social Sciences_executive function_central unit). As a consequence, reforms may be rejected by Algerian academics; '(...) From where does one bring us all these new theories? It can't apply to us; it's imported (...)' (7_m_Arts_Humanities_Social Sciences_executive function_central unit). The result is an expression of their position of personal oscillation.

More broadly, the ambivalence of Algerian higher education internationalisation, in a system characterised by central governance and the lack of institutional autonomy, which is not conducive, is pinpointed:

> (...) there is an ambivalence. Theoretically, the Ministry of Higher Education is supposed to be an orchestra conductor. It is supposed to organise the function, the functions of higher education and to ensure the operation. But while everything that comes out of the nature of the courses, teaching methods, must be left to, teaching methods and even strategies, strategies, strategies, must emanate from universities; Okay. I believe it very sincerely because it is, because it is the university which is in contact with the field, which can say what orientation we can give to higher education; because the Ministry is disconnected from reality; it is a huge, very bureaucratic machine that manipulates figures, that manipulates ideologies. Often,

it's like that, but in reality, in terms of content, it's the field that shows; so, of course, we can imagine an intelligent Ministry which could associate scientific advice, for example by establishments, in the promulgation of policies and strategies. So there is not, it is not vertical. So us, we are there in our universities, we notice a lot of things, and we are a force of proposals (...) (3_f_STEM).

This situation of ambivalent Algerian academia, caught between the national and international in the higher education system, leads to personal oscillation as is reflected below:

(...) Because what is going on; yes, a heavy and universal tendency, which is called democratisation of access to university, that is very good, but that should not prevent us from thinking globally as to how to find excellency while keeping democratisation, of, access to university, yes. The two must... we must think about how to associate the two in fact (...) (1_m_Arts_Humanities_Social_Sciences_research).

Here, there is a plea not to continue to look inwards at the national system, but to assume an international outlook, where this domestic policy objective has no meaning, but actually hampers worldwide competitiveness. Likewise, national higher education policy ought to be reformed before assuming international ambitions, by ranking and standardisation:

I would say that the main challenge has already been to re-establish a basic standard, the fight against a drop of university standards, the fight against plagiarism, the fight against corruption even, I would almost say. I believe that it exists, unfortunately, in particular the corruption of lecturers by students. Okay, yes. To get better grades or ... etc. It is a phenomenon which exists; with drifts sometimes rather unfortunate. The requirement of quality first, above all, before thinking of entering an international standard;

no, rather, hoping to be at a good, international level (...) (1_m_Arts_Humanities_Social Sciences_research).

In contrast, current developments in internationalisation adaptation are sometimes rejected, and it is advised to backtrack to first focus on the national system's flaws, and subsequently, gradually, extend one's focus to the immediate geographical area, i.e., the Maghreb region:

> I was going to say the same thing, but I would add that there is this obsession, I was going to say maybe 'ranking' whatever ... Yes. ...at the international level, which I would say to say does not apply to the current state in Algeria because we should, instead of ... feeding this kind of race ... not even race, I was going to say this ... ... this ... how to say? This illusion of ... from international ranking integration, set goals that are much more realistic and much more ... Yes. Much more, we will say important, go to the current state that is to say that it is really, it is, I think, it is really far from our current concerns than to have wanted to hope to enter these international classifications so, and I think that for the moment in the Algerian case it would be necessary to be inspired by ... perhaps to be inspired by cases which are more within our range, for example to be interested much more in what is happening with our Moroccan or Tunisian neighbours (...) (1_m_Arts_Humanities_Social Sciences_research).

From an Algerian academic's perspective, national higher education policy needs to be conducive towards, and take into account, the international aspect, which is inextricably linked to research: '(...) attributing great importance to documentation. First of all, it's the purchase of documents, books, journals etc., and, at the same time, at the same time, facilitate the implementation of cooperation with research centres, libraries, and abroad (...)' (15_m_Arts_Humanities_Social Sciences_administrative function_faculty). Correspondingly, a STEM researcher said: 'Well... Really need to international setting I mean you cannot live in a close the doors or closed setting for research for technology and so we all the time we work with Europe and think it is going to last for a while' (2_m_STEM_research).

Currently, however, the opposite applies:

> (...) on the other hand, in the teaching sphere. I believe that we remain in an Algerian-Algerian system. Okay. We did not, we did not manage to adopt or to start processes of exchanges and the application of models which are effective in other countries. No. So we remain in an instruction, I would say, a bit traditional, in which, for example, information technologies and the digital struggle to find their place, that's it. So there are these two things. Teaching is, remains traditional, and with a certain delay, which worsens with massification, the level of language, which means 'level of language', so, access to bibliographic resources (...) (3_f_STEM).

It becomes apparent that especially adaptation measures of language requirements fail. Consequently, there is also frustration resulting from the juxtaposition of Algeria as developing country versus the personal position of an internationally (by default) active researcher; '(...) we are in a third world country, underdeveloped (...)' (15_m_Arts_Humanities_Social Sciences_administrative function_faculty). This leads to the following conclusion as a rejection of internationalisation altogether: '(...) so yes, internationalisation, I would almost say that, for the moment, it doesn't make much sense in the Algerian case (...)' (1_m_Arts_Humanities_Social Sciences_research).

5. Academics' Voices: Coping Strategies and Motivations for Research Activity

Algerian academics have adopted a variety of coping strategies to deal with the ambivalences between the national and international focus they are exposed to, as outlined previously, and these strategies become critical in their daily work at the Algerian university or research institute. Further, there are different reasons for each strategy in terms of research engagement, which is classified into three categories, namely, macro, meso and micro-level reasons.

5.1   Research Engagement and Prioritisation

Self-initiative and Personal Motivation

There are tools to enhance quality assurance in research, such as the digitisation of publications for improved transparency, as in this case from the social sciences:

> All publications that we did, the journals, there were only paper journals. Now, all journals, from this year on, all journals will be electronic journals. So, there is more foresight and transparency in the work. Yes, okay. So, it works well? Yes, it must work, because it is a new system, medium that they use, and it is an effective means of control: who does work, who doesn't do it.

However, wider measures aimed at overall institutional evaluation regarding research output are still not assumed by the governing body, or are insufficient, as shown by the following:

> So, the Ministry, I think, has a role to play in it, which requires evaluation commissions of what is done in our

research centres, in our universities. So, the government must assume this role. Yes. To say, to send inspections, that's the role of the Ministry anyway! To inspect, to investigate what is happening, that's it.

Hence, the individual's initiative still counts in the absence of other institutional measures: 'We can assure it internally, we can assure it internally.' Personal motivation, too, is also at the root of extra-curricular activities, such as a 'Nexus for *(institution)* University Network for Innovation and Entrepreneurship', and it is up to the individual Algerian academic to seize opportunities: 'As a researcher, I can tell you that there are quite a few opportunities. Are they exploited at best? I do not think so. I think we can exploit these opportunities better than we do now. But there is a lot of potential; there are a lot of opportunities in research.'

Despite the fact that political engagement may be rejected; 'However, there is one thing that we don't do. It's politics at university. No politics. And that's for the better', policy influence is desired, e.g., in promoting university-industry linkages in applied research in STEM: 'That's why I say: The only thing that, it's the subcontracting at the level of different labs, at the level of research labs and all. Outsourcing certain projects and all, with industry, would be good.' The latter situation presents a personal oscillation by Algerian academics.

Although the Ministry depends on input by those in the academic field, at the institutions, 'Now they are harmonising; to do things technically. But everything must come from the base. And therefore, the Ministry only validates', the feedback solicited sometimes does not bear fruit: 'When there was the director, once she came to *(city)*; she said to me: "We want people to propose something. It's them who don't want to propose".' This resistance might be explained by disagreement with the prevailing policy, for example, in the Bologna process reform adaptation: 'Doing two systems in parallel is a bit schizophrenic; it is not normal. If we decide to go to the future, we go to the future once and for all. We will not say, "Yes, ok,

I maintain that one".' Accordingly, reform willingness and support depend on the individual person's mindset:

> It's mentality. Whether in 72, whether LMD, whether in internationalisation, whether in scientific research, whether in pedagogy, in pedagogical practices, pedagogical practices which use new methodologies, new approaches. I am in (sub-field of discipline), so I was working on (topic related to discipline) etc. And in (humanities disciplines). But (sub-field of discipline) exists in all disciplines. And then, the big changes are in mentalities. If we did, if we succeeded in changing mentalities, that means that we managed to operate and put in place changes.

The insistence on personal initiative also extends to the execution of professional tasks associated in general with the role of academic; 'So, as we say, the seriousness is not everywhere. And anyway, that depends on the conscience of each lecturer', and specifically with regards to interdisciplinarity and openness beyond the strict borders of one's field as a researcher: 'You can, you can solve problems. An economist can do health economics. Society, social sciences could explain the problems that exist. You, see? It's something like that. Well, but people must adapt.' Not least, self-motivation is also decisive in starting and maintaining international cooperation: 'But I managed to formalise the partnership of our research unit with (*university in Spain*), in (*city in Spain*), and it has become an agreement between the two universities, and other disciplines can access it, they can use the advantages of this convention.'

International Sphere Privileged or Practised

The opinions voiced reflect individual Algerian academics' behaviour in engaging in research.

First, members of the Algerian diaspora worldwide are known and praised, even beyond their discipline, as shown by the following statement from a humanities background:

There are researchers who do, who have talent, who have been able to impose themselves globally, in the United States, in Japan. I quote in Japan Mohamed Banat who put in question a small theory, a small theory in physics, which dates from the 19th century! Fluid mechanics. And the theory, it was we have Senhadji, concerning research from here and in France; we have Zerhouni in the United States in medical imaging, and who had become, who was appointed by the Americans as the director of the medical center, of the first medical institution in the world, researching medicine globally. So, it's a source of pride for Algeria.

Likewise, Algerian colleagues' achievements abroad are acknowledged; however, with the comment that they do not return at all or return to leave again to then continue benefiting other countries:

I hope that the Algerians of the diaspora play this role of high standards here locally. But unfortunately, they do not return. That's it. And those who returned; among them brilliant people, left because they were discouraged, I am thinking of the great Algerian inventor. Yes. Belgacem Haba, who is from Biskra; who was in Silicon Valley as an inventor, as a scientist, and who was in the ranking of the 100 best inventors in the world; he was placed 40th, who came back for pure, really, I would say... Willingness? Desire to change things here, in Biskra. Of course, it was, it was a disaster, and he was taken, I would say, literally drafted, by the Japanese; who came to see him in Algeria; to offer him a job there in Japan. And he went back to Japan. So ... and this man, Belgacem Haba, has created an association, one finds the site on the internet, of Algerians, Algerian scientists from the diaspora. Yes, yes. You can go and see. Very good. And so, we see the great willingness of this man, to try to create a dynamic. Yes. And another who is famous, Noureddine Melikechi, who is at NASA. Yes. And who is one of the people in charge of the MARS 2020 programme, so the exploration of the planet Mars for 2020, him too, I see him at times here to lecture, try to get a little involved with the students, send a message. But the result is always the same. All those who can leave, leave, and don't come back.

Accordingly, the emigration wave in the 1990s saw many members of the Algerian academia leave without adequate replacement in the following decade; 'Listen, the potential, at one point, we had good lecturers; at one point. But with the braised years, it was the 90s, yes, many lecturers left Algeria. And the next generation, it's not well done.' Today, emigration continues at a high level; 'Algeria is one of the worst cases in Africa, especially, I believe we are the second country in Africa in terms of brain drain. So, there is a state of mind of flight, finally, of abandonment.' Still, the situation is different insofar as the younger generation is seeking better research conditions: 'I prefer Europe yes, yes, I prefer Europe. *Why?* Because it's a developed country, it's developed countries, it's countries that encourage doctoral students, researchers, that's it.'

Furthermore, non-domestically available infrastructure and equipment are cited in prioritising research abroad, even if temporary: 'You go abroad for a month; you finish something; you come here, you have a problem, because the material is there; you can't use it.' Algerian academics also encourage their PhD candidates to seek opportunities abroad where there is funding: 'Students, there is mobility, too, they can, of course, benefit from these stays there, doctoral candidates ... *Doctoral candidates.* Doctoral students, they have access, and they even have the possibility of; 50% of the budgets allocated to these stays are reserved for these doctoral students', thus capitalising on their own positive experiences abroad in being able to gain knowledge to apply at home, such as: 'Well, we are a bit of a cliché of the French model, it must be said. But it is true that there were, how do I say, services, that I found there, that exist here. And I, personally, when I return, I, how to say, well, I try to apply what I learned there, I try to apply it here. Then I propose to my manager, I make a report and all that.'

Adhering to National Principles

Algerian academics' personal reasons for engaging in research may also relate to language, authority, and values. These factors are reflected in the following sample statements in the sense that Algerian academics may orient or prioritise their research because of a certain national interest, which, in this case, applies to Arabised disciplines.

> In principle, there must be. The Ministry must make sure that orientation must be according to our needs. We will not direct students towards a field which does not interest us, for example, an area that would interest Alaska, it does not interest us. An example. Or, an area that would interest maybe South Africa may not interest us. So, orientation, I think it is the Ministry which takes charge (...)

They may also feel compelled to do research, or a certain type of research, as part of their perceived duties as a university academic, or, indeed, to comply with economic directives: 'Algerian university research has evolved a lot, simply because the state has put the means. Of course, we are not a; that is to say, we have not reached them, the desired expectations by our Ministry.'

5.2 Limited Research Activity

Macro Level: Governance Reasons – Lack of Budget and Human Resources Autonomy

Algerian higher education governance is characterised by centralisation and associated administrative structures, explained thus: 'We manage research projects, we manage research projects through our research entities which are, let's say, mandated for this kind of management, such as research agencies.' Accordingly, there is little autonomy for individual researchers: 'And these research activities, automatically, they are carried out within a research laboratory.' The latter opinion is criticised by pointing out that 'We must create an entity centrally, and leave the freedom to these structures to create the sub-structures they would like.'

The importance of hierarchical structures, too, is emphasised: 'I can even discuss with, and I have had to talk to the director. But I cannot go beyond, because it stops, my task if you want. So that's it, anyway, I do solicit anyway, I make an appeal to the people who are there for this task. And a little, hierarchically speaking, for my superior.' This individual scenario also applies at the institutional level: 'Well, it depends on ... Because sometimes, the formalisation of your contacts takes a long time. The university always requests the advice of the Ministry; it can take some time.'

Although flexibility is possible, as is shown in the following: 'When there is a research topic or a field of promoted research, and if the regulations disturb or hinder, we always try to contact our authority to have exceptions, to do or correct the scope for this area there, and it is done', in general, government control is viewed as an obstacle by academics: 'So, it's an administration, although it's light, but it's still an administration, heavy enough for us, to implement things.' This status quo has repercussions on research; 'And now scientific research, for sure, is encountering democratic difficulties; administrative difficulties, but it's on the right track.' Thus, it is openly admitted that the issue lies within governance structures: 'So on the teaching side, on the training, research side, it is done. But on the governance side, according to the people.'

Frustration caused by delays due to budgeting restrictions are evident, as in this case; 'Everything works very well, but when it comes, because it is a job where the money is spent, it's been more than two years that nothing has been done.' These then point towards the lack of autonomy, encompassing budgetary as well as staff decisions; 'Recruitment, it's complicated, because civil service no longer recruits; the state has no money left,' which impedes not only international initiatives: ''We wanted to do an Erasmus + (*name programme*) on that. At least to draw up the programme.

Afterwards, we didn't have time. *Right, that's the problem.* The problem, it's human resources. Very few human resources', but also impedes university-industry linkages that play a role in STEM applied research: 'As we are not autonomous, and as companies need a speed of reaction which is high, that's it. So if you want a university-business relationship, it really has to be something autonomous, with its own budget, etc., etc..' Consequently, these linkages are difficult to establish and maintain.

Challenges of Academic Freedom in the Social Sciences

The prevailing governance system is perceived to have a negative impact on the social sciences in particular: 'To say: they were looking for what they called social peace, but social peace is not, everything is... I wanted to apply the regulation; it was bad. So, actually: "To not have any problems, let all of them pass".' Here, the political ideology of socialism is said to be instrumentalised as a means of control – the regulation of social peace to be applied by lecturers, meaning that competency of students is secondary in the assessment.

Lack of Appreciation of Research (Outcomes)

The fact that there is an issue with attributing and labelling expert status points to a lack of appreciation of research outcomes: 'They are experts. Except that, we need to label them experts, to appreciate them.' Likewise, ways to exit academia in favour of the private sector may be sought in applied technical fields, as in the following case: 'In IT too, it works, in Telecom, too. Yes, Telecom, like in France. There are trainings that allow you to get out of it.'

Insufficiency of Competent Doctoral Candidates or Post-docs

The lack of, or inadequacy of, qualified human resources as a paramount component regarding junior members of a research unit is described by a STEM representative. Reasons for the unsatisfactory status are portrayed as a contemporary problem:

> Yes, the succession has not been assured. Me, in any case, we have young lecturers recruited, but they are recruited after having completed the trajectory we are actually criticising right now, that means with all the linguistic, structural, methodological weaknesses. And all that, so, it is not done, for … I'm sorry, I paint you a blackboard. It is not done to hope to raise the level.

For academic staff, the need for capacity-building and training has either not been identified or remains uncatered for: 'Even if, personally, I said that, at times, I provide some training for the staff, tasks. Still, it must be remembered that there is a real lack of training, significant recycling, that's it. Before, we spoke about globalisation. How can staff improve without having training, too?' In addition, there is this view:

> So the recycling of information can be included in this framework of conventions. OK. So it can be included, it would be very beneficial, I would say, for this staff, for this staff, who is thirsty to perform, who is all alert. If one trains its staff, we have a service that is really… Up to date (laughs)

The lack of capacity in doctoral candidates, in particular, leads to frustration: 'There is no transfer of knowledge. No, they are not used to learning how to reflect, they are like that, and they learn the exercises, and so, that translates into this somewhat discouraging level at university.' The consequence of this situation is favouring junior foreign researchers altogether: 'I don't want to run after Algerians. That, it's my opinion. It's useless.'

Meso Level: Institutional Challenges – Lack or insufficiency of Infrastructure and Equipment

At the institutional level, Algerian academics face obstacles in research due to infrastructural challenges. Those might be in the form of library opening hours: 'I give you an example. At one point, we said: "The library, we do not work at the library because it is not open". OK, we are not Harvard; we are not...'. Notably, the situation has deteriorated since the introduction of the Bologna system; 'This is among the advantages of Bologna *(laughs)* because before, with the old system, *(institutional unit)* working hours were from 8:30 a.m. until 8 p.m. Now, with the new system, it's 8:30 a.m. until 6 p.m.' Further, especially in STEM, there is a lack of equipment in laboratories, leading to idleness:

> No, I think there have been means that have been deployed, well, it must be said that, when we deploy certain means, we wait too long. The proof is, at the level of the research lab, we had some material which we cannot use yet because something is missing or lack of something else, or we were moved etc. So, that blocks a researcher.

Once more, working conditions abroad are perceived and portrayed as more favourable.

Heavy Teaching Load

A heavy teaching load also prevents a professor from engaging in research. One reason is the generational change, with too few new academics, following a wave of retirement in the older generation.

> And others who have left, gone for retirement in quite large numbers. And so, the number of staff has decreased, and that of the students has increased. It is like talking about the offer and the demand. So, there was a slight difference in the balance. At times, we can't, I would say, for example, provide a service, since the workforce is missing, you see? The workforce is missing. It's a bit that, it's ... We had some obstacles in this, with regards to this situation.

Further, the status quo is problematic for young researchers, who are not allowed to develop their research portfolio and profile, in the arts and humanities, as this example shows:

> I have the impression from what I hear, that there may be an overload of lessons; at master and doctorate levels,

which in my opinion, but it may be the opinion of someone who is old- school, which in my opinion, is not necessarily the best thing to do, because that, arriving at this stage of training, requires great autonomy of the researcher: do not overload with lectures or work, but rather let one focus on research and the, I would say, even maybe the development of one's own methodological tools.

Micro Level: Personal Reasons – Lack of Interest in Reform Implementation or Adaptation

On a personal level, there exists resistance to implement or adapt to the Bologna process, as is by the following example:

And so, among the failures and the reasons for failure, not 100% failure, but there were some flaws in this system: it is, the students did not follow, and until now, they do not follow, and also the lecturers, some lecturers did not want to get involved; did not make any efforts, especially the older generation. Ah, the old ones, they don't like it, because this system is based on learning, and also on new technologies, ICT, it's very important. We cannot do a course without, for example, using a beamer with the LMD. Though I noticed, at the level of the faculty, for example, I would say the young people are better adapted to this system than the lecturers. Until now, some oppose this LMD system.

Another example is the reluctance to leave one's comfort zone, as in this case:

And sometimes I did meetings with the lecturers and things went wrong. There are people who always refused the... Yes, yes. Yes, they thought it was complicated, especially those who taught engineering and everything. At one point, I do not remember, there is someone I do not know what, I would have explained the principle, and on the side, I said a sentence that people didn't like very much. I told them: 'Excuse me, you have to re-format your brains'. Yes! That's clear (laughs), I can imagine, yes. That's it: 'Re-format your brains. The world will change, you have to apply it'

Others personally reject the notion of the reform because of its lack of suitability or local applicability:

So, on the other hand, the big objectives, so, that the LMD had to achieve, have already been achieved with the reform of 71. Thirdly, the LMD could not stick to the Algerian university, because the main principles of the LMD, they were made for Europe, they weren't made for Arab countries or for African countries. You see?

This view is also shared by a STEM representative, although there is some confidence that things will improve over time;

When it comes to weaknesses, we are all the time behind schedule. We have massification which is not good. The programmes don't really solve local problems, and these are the weaknesses that we have to look at. Also, maybe the system will have the LMD issue (unclear 00:52:03-6) Okay, yeah. That is one of the things I would say at least give one more year so you will have a better setting.

Due to a lack of strategy and orientation, the two systems still co-exist, which forces academics to struggle and strive for individual solutions out of necessity: ''I gave you'. But: 'Don't give me, give me my rights, and leave me alone'. So, that is, there are a lot of things that we should still review in these systems. I haven't been out since (*beginning of the 2010s*) with their system. I was out until last year. But, by my own system, if I am going to ... .' Consequently, confusion persists: 'We do it, but we remained very classic. For a few years, we stayed in the old system, with labels, with a discourse of the new system, but people were struggling to change, to adapt.'

Lack of, or Over-reliance on, Institutional Knowledge

In the context of difficult access to information and malfunctioning communication in Algerian higher education

‒ 'The university could better communicate internally and externally. So, this is a, the first problem I see, it's a communication problem' ‒ as stated from the perspective of a central unit executive, there might be a lack of information, impeding international collaboration during research visits:

· It stopped, or it's a bit hidden. That, I don't know, we don't have any information, at all, not at all. We don't have it. Even if we ask, even if, I said, personally, I went to France, it's been 2 years, and I was asked if we came as part of a convention? And all that. I came back, I asked, I asked; I didn't have one; after all, I was told there was none, it wasn't there, that was it.

However, the governing body, represented by the institution, has an authority that may not be questioned: 'I believe that there is, the role of the authority, it is important. We need a roof; we need a papa, we need... (...) When we are in the public sector, there is massification, there is free education, there is all that. But when one has the authority, it is important. It is important, an authority which is aware.'

Non-incentive by (Additional) Salary

The fact that research activity is not normally remunerated beyond the salary corresponding to one's staff rank in the Algerian higher education context is a factor that may deter academics, especially younger ones, from engaging in research, even though the conditions and facilities might be favourable.

> So, you ask them: go, now that you don't have the stress of the PhD, that's it, there is a device here, it costs a million dollars, and I'm not exaggerating. We even have a device that costs 1,5 million dollars. Go to work, take the doc, read it, explain to me that you have understood, and we will start it. Good luck! Good luck. It's an example.

Hence, concerning STEM, more economically attractive options in the industry are sought. However, the occasional existence of additional remuneration attracts considerable interest, which is however motivated by the financial incentive only, as reported below:

> An example, an example. A month ago, the Ministry launched research projects. These research projects are to allow for doctoral training, but at the same time, the researcher is paid on the project. It's not huge. But he is paid. As if by chance, people disappear, when they hear projects, they come back, they are interested in doing projects. They do not propose the project; they don't come up with the idea, they don't offer to work on it; just to be a member of the project.

Lack of Personal Connections in an Informal System

The dependency on personal connections to be able to publish, and be published, is described in the following statement from an arts perspective:

> It's in terms of analysis, you see, in terms; for example, I give you a very simple example. You write an article, in which you will defend, for example, you will defend the Salafism, Islamism. You know, if you don't know, for example, the person in charge of the issue of the journal, or if you don't know the editor, or if you don't know, or if you do not don't have an entry point, chances are high that your paper won't pass.

Therefore, especially in the social sciences, where ideology has been shown to play a major role, those informal criteria may override scientific quality, with the consequence of no publishing activity.

Lack of Competencies Including Language Issues

Regarding the personal skills of individual Algerian academics, although communication issues are also mentioned as obstacles, the lack or inadequacy of necessary English-language skills is most prominent; 'For the simple reason that people don't take communication seriously. I stayed for fifteen years, trying to find solutions. We did; I was in a centre for lecturer training. That's where I learned how to communicate. So, normally all lecturers should have that background.' This lack of English-language skills is increasingly seen as a handicap in the default international sphere of academia: 'It remains a language problem. It's still a language problem; it's a language problem', as stated by a STEM representative. This view is shared by humanities representatives, too: 'Yes, English. We have a language handicap; we don't master English well, that's why we prefer to go.'

In this context, the continued orientation towards French, including in the otherwise Arabised social sciences, and more so for the older generation, is at the root of this issue:

> You know, the French model existed because France had set up the Algerian university. Algiers, it was a big city, but above all, Algiers, it was centralised in Algiers. Later, there was the establishment of several universities in the big cities, first. Then in the provinces, etc. But we stayed on the French model because the competence had attended their training during the French time. It was a little bit natural; it was natural. It is, either instructors, lecturers who were trained in France, or who were trained in Algeria during the French era, either... That means that the competence was in French. This is why hard sciences have continued to be taught in French because we have this reference that exists, and the reference, either in terms of lecturers or in terms of documentation, was French.

This state of affairs is reiterated by a social sciences colleague: '(...) in our generation. We were all only francisants (laughs), only francisants.'

Given these circumstances, academics are struggling to produce scientific work, and, hence publish, in particular in the STEM disciplines; e.g., 'I write in English, yes. Before, no, before, it was in French. My dissertation, it was in French. Everything in French. Now, it's completely different. I translate. That's the solution. I download articles; I translate them into French after I can, I do what I want. If not in English, no.' However, likewise, the use of Arabic may impede a researcher's inclusion and access, especially in the arts and humanities; '(...) in history, in archaeology, in philosophy, in Arabic. Because everything is written in Arabic, in law, everything is done in Arabic. So, there may be some extraordinary topics that may interest the Americans, the Germans, but they are not visible.'

5.3   Alternatives in Academia

There is also a third coping strategy, of not choosing either of the strategies above, and not positioning oneself altogether, by striving for alternatives in academia in the form of administrative or supervisory roles. Outreach may also be a priority or a preference. Three main types of alternatives can be distinguished: devoting oneself to lecturing, to supervising, or to taking on an executive position. University self-administration in general – even with the limited institutional autonomy in the Algerian context – is positively underlined, as in this case from the humanities; 'What is good, what is nice at university, around the world, is that those responsible are lecturers. That is, those who ensure administration.'

A teaching focus in the arts is emphasised as follows: 'I let the student come, I offer him a panoply of things, and you will see that they can ... that the students can offer us extraordinary things. We must not impose things too much.' Teaching in the humanities and social sciences also encompasses the transmission of broader, general knowledge; 'train them artistically; train them philosophically; teach them to think.' One might even go so far as to hold the lecturer chiefly responsible for study and even research outcomes: 'The success of the training, I will go further, the success of scientific production begins with the genius of the lecturer, it is him who stimulates, it is him who encourages, it is him who motivates, it is him who promotes these thinking heads.'

In STEM, the supervisory role has, for example, expressions such as: '(...) but still, we see the difference. In the 90s, for example, there were thesis defences once every three months, four months, there is a one. Whereas now, there are defences practically every week.' In addition, there is a need for training, which must be assumed but which is currently not yet the case: 'For the university the solution exists, it is 'hire the best'. We must have, we must be more selective, and also, do internal training. *For that, time is needed.* A lot of time is needed; it takes time; it takes dedicated staff. That's the problem.' Postgraduate students have also recently been integrated into research units, as this example from STEM shows: 'Because now, the master and doctorate are part of the activities of research laboratories.' In parallel, funding has been provided: 'And, also, these days, we have enough research labs, we have had extraordinary funding for a few years now. And this funding has enabled us to acquire equipment. And this equipment has enabled us to have certain doctorates defend.' Hence, academics are called upon more to exercise their supervisory role.

The executive position may be adopted, for example, in a dean's role, as in STEM: 'So these lecturers must be managed, they must be managed, by whom? By the Dean each time, so there are problems.' More broadly, managerial tasks may be seen as integral to any academic endeavour on its various levels.

6. Implications for Higher Education Policy in the Arab World and Global South

The scope of these recommendations encompasses a personal contribution to Algeria, where stakeholders and political representatives have been approached and their views solicited in interviews. In English, the recommendations offer not only new international accessibility, but an alternative, outsider, and thus potentially more neutral and credible perspective, to be consulted on a stand-alone basis. The focus on opportunities rather than problems is characteristic of a new mentality oriented towards good practices, quality assurance, research cooperation, and the acknowledgement of non-African academics' training in Africa rather than the traditional vice-versa model, which implies a certain disadvantageous power dynamic as an expression of neo-colonial structural violence. On the contrary, while there is currently little activity in terms of training non-Africans in Africa, there is a lot of potential and scope for future endeavours. Objectives of policy recommendations in the higher education field can be more broadly subsumed under quality assurance, since a causal link can be established between quality development and higher education institution development and management (Schmidt, 2007).

Consequently, policy recommendations regarding the Algerian higher education system are derived from the empirical research in this study in that the micro-level observations from the data analysis in the previous chapters are employed to link to the macro level. They are thematically structured into five categories, addressing the macro as well as micro perspective, and introducing an autonomous decision-making meso level (the institutional level), which does not exist yet. In a nutshell, higher education institutions are special organisations, and the academic sphere is, globally, characterised by self-governance as a prerequisite for its functioning, even though it is not the default case worldwide at present. Therefore, conditions need to be put in place that allow for a university's research function to operate as its core, inextricably linked to increasing internationalisation and regionalisation of higher education. Centralised governance and ideological considerations informing higher education policy choices limit progress in the sense of participation and visibility, as they are nationally oriented and have a negative impact on the desired continuing transition into a knowledge society, which restricts academic freedom as described above.

In Algeria, this process enjoys a high priority of an education-related budget, equality in access and quasi full participation, human resources, strong and publicly funded institutions, resulting in well-qualified staff and competency-based training of the young population as next-generation professionals and executives. In this context, Algeria, which already hosts numerous international students, mostly from sub-Saharan countries, may share its experience as so-called 'best-practices' in dealing with globalisation impacts in higher education. Other African as well as Arab countries, and beyond, including the Asia-Pacific region, Europe, and the Americas, are also included. The expected, soon-to-be-established private universities will likely increase competition and offer quality assurance, among other perspectives, by benchmarking with international higher education institutions and frameworks (Sebihi & Schoelen, 2019).

6.1 Knowledge Management and Research Practices

Before research practices and processes can occur, knowledge management is a necessity. A culture of exchange is a prerequisite, which needs to be established, e.g., by academic societies and conferences. Algerian understanding to date revolves around physical laboratories, experiments, and number and type of publications. It mostly concerns applied research and is thus heavily biased towards STEM fields when compared with the social sciences, arts and humanities. This thesis has shown that there are a variety of obstacles preventing university academic staff from engaging more actively in research. Also, it is noteworthy that innovations have not been mentioned in interviews, which was the expectation, from talking to researchers about research. Therefore, there need to be reform elements for a transformation into a research and knowledge culture. While teaching currently prevails in practice, assuming that research activity is first and foremost intrinsically motivated, and thus individual, since Algeria is in a position to re-allocate its generous education-related funding, the country may:

- Define national research programmes and priorities in a participatory manner, including non-state and industry representatives, and review as appropriate;
- Establish a framework, i.e., in the form of standing and ad hoc committees, where relevant stakeholders are involved in commissioning, using and evaluating research, as well as in the development of strategies and systems for knowledge management and sharing;
- Prioritise a knowledge base of state-of-the-art research and sustained investment in interdisciplinary research to develop new methodologies and theories from critical inquiry and innovative spirit as the foundational understanding of research;
- Disseminate research funding nationally as well as internationally by electronic means rather than publishing only.

With regards to promoting and incentivising individual research activity, measures include:

- Create the legal basis for the status of the researcher;
- Reduce (undergraduate) teaching load by introducing more specialised courses, and employing needs-based teaching assistants;
- Facilitate, and streamline the roll-out of, a sabbatical year or semester;

- Assess publications on the principle of quality over quantity, to be taken into consideration for staff ranking as well;
- Involve all national research centres in doctoral education in collaboration with universities and create pathways for staff exchanges and visiting lecturers;
- Implement individual, non-state research funding possibilities;
- Implement English-language support and funding for translations, with a focus on the social sciences, arts and humanities;
- Acknowledge personal science communication activities as 'third-mission' public events.

6.2 Post-graduate-level Research Training and Standardisation

Another central issue identified by this thesis is the need for the development of researchers' competencies, or the lack of research students' competencies, especially with regards to a scientific working approach. This extends to the use of foreign languages, English in particular. To avoid unsystematic, individualised training of doctoral candidates as has been reported as being common practice, it is proposed to:

- Discontinue centralised PhD entrance national exams (*concours*) and quotas for the number of PhD candidates in scientific disciplines, and instead grant freedom of choice to researchers to take on PhD candidates according to the potential for research ability and innovation;
- Introduce institution-wide and interdisciplinary or discipline-specific mandatory skills courses in foreign languages, research methodology, academic writing, presentation and communication competences, research ethics, e.g., by a doctoral school, and create peer coaching encounters;
- Encourage empirical research designs for data collection critical for quality assurance;

- Procure specialist research equipment as a national competitive advantage;
- Provide or enhance research support structures, such as the availability of literature, including online access, extend library opening hours, and facilitate the importation of equipment.

6.3 National and International Collaboration and Partnership

Owing to negligible staff exposure to internationalisation and comparatively scarce mobility opportunities to date, there is a need for more international awareness, hosting of international academics in Algeria, and a greater Algerian presence abroad, to increase the present overall low scientific visibility:

- Start/promote national disciplines or subject associations with annual conferences;
- Distribute national and international academic events equally throughout the national territory to include and promote the South;
- Strengthen regional exchange in the Maghreb by networks, such as the Bologna Process, and facilitate student and staff mobility and agree on accreditation standards;
- Wherever feasible, encourage co-supervision arrangements, co-publish, and invite international colleagues to take part in doctoral defence juries, as well as actively seek these opportunities from the Algerian side;
- Showcase and promote regional specialist areas of studies of international interest in the humanities, such as Tamazight, Arabic language and literature, Islamic theology, archaeology, medieval and ancient history;
- Reorientate and increase awareness of partnership strategies towards the African continent, the Middle East, and Asian countries, rather than Europe and North America;

- Offer intensive or accompanying Arabic/dialectal/Tamazight as foreign language courses as well as cultural summer school experiences;
- Conceptualise a participatory higher education internationalisation strategy and implementation plan, analogous to the existing five-year plans, and prepare for its application and implementation in institutions;
- Include the diaspora as facilitator and mediator between higher education institutions and countries;
- Join regional bodies and international institutions as associate entities of the UN system.

6.4   University Administration and Leadership

The issues of university staffing and leadership rarely came up in the interviews overall, even though several representatives held administrative, including executive, positions. In contrast, teaching was mentioned throughout. This finding leads to the observation that roles in administration and leadership are not sufficiently fulfilled or are not given priority. Hence, there is a need for capacity-building for incumbents, by training, onboarding and backstopping. On an autonomous meso level, positions, roles and responsibilities have to be defined, and on a macro level, governing structure adaptations and constitutional provisions have to be made.

Institutional Autonomy

Research, excellence and international competitiveness require a supportive environment, which has been reiterated by the findings in this thesis. Hence, institutional autonomy is an essential condition, i.e., the transfer of governance from the centralised body to universities. Concrete measures may take the form of:

- Facilitate transitions between institutions, including flexible admission procedures and guidance, credit accumulation and transfer, and accredited equivalency schemes;

- Reform administrative processes, such as staff recruitment and procurement;
- Allow, and encourage, national profiling of institutions, e.g., research-intensive, professional-oriented, or international foreign-language instruction;
- Begin operations to allow for fee-charging private, including international, higher education providers;
- Create and adequately remunerate administrative-only positions, both on an executive/rectorate level, as well as in faculties or departments;
- Create dedicated international offices within institutions as well as research centres;
- Facilitate academic visits from foreigners by giving institutions the necessary administrative competencies and authorisations;
- Allow income-generation activities, e.g., by university-integrated or affiliated foreign language institutes, research laboratories and spin-offs;
- Establish institutionally multi-faceted services, i.e., quality assurance and monitoring and evaluation units

Strategic Planning Culture

- Conceptualise a mission and a vision for national higher education;
- Engage in, for example, 5-year development plans for higher education;
- Align higher education with other national strategic plans, such as economic and social policy;
- Develop policies consistent with technical and vocational education and employment policy fields, among others;
- Introduce a regulatory framework to define the roles, responsibilities, duties, and rights of stakeholders in higher education;
- Issue guidelines rather than decrees only;

6.5 Infrastructure and Resources

The findings of this thesis highlight that institutional and individual infrastructure is generally sufficient for its purpose, and that resources are available. However, there is a mismatch in what is required, and mismanagement and lack of communication in what is delivered. Academics are confronted with centrally commissioned, standardised physical laboratory provisions rather than an allocation based on individual requests and need assessment. Due to the lack of equipment warranty, insurance, and also administrative support, as well as technicians and maintenance personnel, especially in STEM fields, experimental teaching and research are de facto discouraged because it is challenging to conduct and maintain. In line with institutional autonomy, budget decision-making powers need to be on the meso level, and adapted, e.g., to student numbers. Investments may then be channelled towards human resources and development.

6.6 Digitisation implementation

Higher education institutions worldwide have moved online by necessity, being confronted with the Covid-19 pandemic at the beginning of 2020. For Algeria, there is a great potential for embracing, adopting, and sustainably implementing digitisation for its system as follows:

- Technological education tools, such as Student Management System (SMS) and Learning Management System (LMS) applications, considerably reduce time spent on administrative tasks, presently routinely carried out by academic staff;
- Critical multi-faceted skills such as project management, foreign languages, as well as specialist software requirements, and, as applicable, entrepreneurship may be deployed, learned and taught online;
- Conceptualise a virtual Community of Practice (CoP) as an inclusive platform to share best practices and encourage interdisciplinary exchange for academic staff nationally, and, potentially, internationally;

· Overcome literature access challenges by decentralisation of traditional subscription to, and the provision of, digital journals, eBooks, and other scientific sources. Instead, allocate needs-based budgets to university libraries and national research centres;
· Use blended learning approaches to ensure location-independent and gender-balanced equity of access;
· Implement remote lecturing possibilities to involve, and reach out to, the diaspora;
· Use online conferencing technology to facilitate co-supervision arrangements, thesis defences, and research collaboration, including conference presentations;
· Offer Massive Open Online Courses (MOOCs) on established international platforms, and prepare an Arab education space, offering courses in both Arabic and English;
· Promote improved worldwide visibility for Algerian academic staff by an open access policy, i.e., make theses as well as *OPU* academic publications freely available online.

6.7 Benchmarking and Quality Assurance

The main outcome of the data analysis is the need for better quality, and systematic quality assurance, in higher education.

Benchmarking Arab and African Countries

Algeria is culturally influenced by both Arab League and African Union member states. This dual position presents an opportunity to benefit from to both contexts. To account for, and eventually achieve, systemic change, a holistic approach has to be adopted. In an African context, national higher education revitalisation has been noted, recently, based on four case studies in Western and Southern Africa (United Nations University, 2009), albeit from a practitioners' rather than a theoretical, foundation perspective. At its foundation are good or so-called best practices; however, there is no systematic quality assurance, strategic planning, operational planning, or implementation and monitoring to date.

This trend, however, is in contrast to Algeria's higher education policy status quo, largely drawing on reform ideas and influences from Europe, especially France, and North America. To streamline its endeavours in higher education advancement, Algeria should consult and align its policies with existing continental or regional strategies, namely, the African Union's *Agenda 2063*[1], the *Continental Education Strategy for Africa* (CESA) 2016-2025[2], the *Science, Technology, and Innovation Strategy for Africa* (STISA) 2024[3] , the *Arab Strategy for Science, Technology and Innovation* (ASSTI)[4] and the associated *Executive Plan*[5]. Furthermore, Algeria needs to consider the progress of implementation measures of SDG no. 4, Education[6], which currently does not play a major role, as can be seen by its absence from political discourse and strategy papers.

Benchmarking should also be practised with cooperative countries, however, less with the so-called global North. In the Arab world, Jordan has invested immensely in its national higher education system. It has strategically internationalised and put quality assurance rather than quantification on the policy agenda. Therefore, Jordan could serve as a case to be replicated – more precisely, its strategies and roadmap for higher education reform (Khader, 2009).

At the beginning of this study, the idea was to compare the Algerian with the South African transitional situation to assess positioning and strategies to deal with challenges in the respective higher education systems, and to showcase continental best practices to allow for more likely acceptance. In South Africa, being a widely accepted African continental

---

1   https://au.int/en/agenda2063/overview
2   https://au.int/sites/default/files/documents/29958-doc-cesa__-__english-v9.pdf
3   https://au.int/sites/default/files/newsevents/workingdocuments/33178-wd-stisa-english__-__final.pdf
4   http://www.fasrc.org/uploads/Arab%20Strategy.pdf (available in Arabic only)
5   http://www.fasrc.org/uploads/Arab%20Strategy%20Plan.pdf (available in Arabic only)
6   https://sustainabledevelopment.un.org/sdg4

reference, less risk of politicisation was to be expected. The Southern African experience of decolonisation and transition from the racist apartheid system towards social inclusion and democratisation of higher education has improved its educational outlook. Assessment and strategic planning has been reflected in several related strategies, among others, its *Ten-Year Innovation Plan*[7], updated by a recent *White Paper on Science, Technology, and Innovation*[8] from 2018, and, most topically, the national strategy for the fourth Industrial Revolution (Sutherland, 2020). More so, in the Southern African Development Community (SADC) region of which South Africa is a member, there has been a focus on higher education institutional quality assurance, beginning as early as 2010 (Ncube, 2010; Rauschmayer et al., 2010).

Overall, the prevailing Algerian orientation towards European and North American countries should not be discontinued but should be reduced in favour of its neighbours and the African continent. The advantage of this approach will be to learn about the challenges, avoid repeating similar mistakes, and initiate reforms.

National Higher Education System Quality Assurance

Existing quality assurance instruments, namely, the *CIAQES* and the *RNAQES*[9] , ought to be revised and adapted to the local context, as the current versions were mainly influenced by European standards and processes, in the form of rather generic and global-oriented consultants' workshops without intercultural elements, and thus do not account for the micro level. Therefore, it is suggested that the Algerian higher education system:

---

7   https://www.sagreenfund.org.za/wordpress/wp-content/
     uploads/2015/04/10-Year-Innovation-Plan.pdf
8   Draft version: https://www.gov.za/sites/default/files/gcis_
     document/201809/41909gon954.pdf
9   La Commission d'Implémentation d'un système
     d'Assurance Qualité dans les établissements
     d'Enseignement Supérieur/Référentiel National de
     l'Assurance Qualité.

- Establishes a national system for quality assurance with the participation of academic staff and relevant stakeholders;
- Introduces objectives, standards, and outcomes with indicators to measure progress and performance;
- Establishes national guidelines for implementation including feedback mechanisms with accessible evaluation results;
- Includes both internal and external self-assessment in the quality assurance plan/ framework to allow for effective monitoring.

6.8 Stakeholder Participation and Involvement

In the recent tense political environment of the so-called *hirak* protest movement, stabilisation of the region is of utmost importance, not least for European countries dealing with issues related to increased migration. Therefore, there is a need for a joint strategy and partnership in graduate employability and labour market relevance of curricula and training. The present Algerian higher education system – as has been described and as is shown by the findings in this work – is characterised by the almost complete absence of non-academic community stakeholders, i.e., the private sector, non-state organisations, and the local institutional environment. These external stakeholders can be meaningfully involved, contribute to the funding, and improve national and international recognition and effectiveness of academic training as well as applied research. The current top-down governance structure needs to be reformed towards a service-oriented approach to take labour market demands into account, for instance. The lack of, or non-availability of data should be counteracted by national surveys and research.

The related specific measures proposed are:

- Create a guiding framework to develop and assess entrepreneurship in the field of higher education;

- Conceptualise a university 'third mission' strategy as well as implementation plan to account for university-society relations;
- Introduce Industrial Advisory Panels (IAPs) and representatives in institutional governing bodies to ensure relevance and topicality of curricula for the needed skills match, including improved graduate employability and placement success;
- Enhance local community relations by targeted events, such as open days, and decentralised recruitment, especially for administrative staff;
- Set up quarterly or semestrial meetings with the local authorities to discuss concerns and voice interests and needs, such as an environment conducive to business;
- Scale up existing pioneering offices of university–industry relationships at institutional or administrative unit (*Wilaya*) level;
- Prioritise and employ national start-ups and small and medium enterprises from university graduates for the required technical as well as service roll-out of higher education digitalisation.

7. From Ambivalences to Hybridisation

The knowledge gaps identified in the course of this work, within the scope of special interest, concern the role and influence of language in higher education and related policy analyses, internal governance structures, decision-making processes below the institutional executive level, as well as student affairs. There is also a lack of statistics, e.g., of graduate (un)employment, as indicated in several interviews, so there is a need for quantitative studies to cover the region, age group, and type of diploma. Furthermore, there are no graduate follow-up studies at present. The Algerian system is also a highly interesting case for quality development, quality assurance implementation, organisational development-related theoretical approaches, and governance trends observed elsewhere in the last decade, such as new public management (NPM), and, more recently, bureaucratic politicisation. Overall, Algeria has the potential to become a reference point for French and Arabic-speaking African, as well as Arab countries, as well as others undergoing similar transition processes. These include increasing higher education internationalisation, social pressure resulting from massified higher education access, youth and graduate unemployment, and migration movements.

Research concerning the classical 'third mission' involving stakeholders external to academia, university-society interactions, industry involvement, as well as issues arising from higher education internationalisation developments, such as mobility patterns, does exist; however, it must be updated, include non-STEM disciplines, and be complemented by more qualitative approaches. The role that non-university institutions of higher education play in the Algerian system, such as the various écoles, is yet to be explored, too, not least in the elite selection and graduate employability research. Likewise, private higher education providers, including curricula content and development, are yet to be taken up in research agendas.

Given its plurilingual character, with the presence of modern standard Arabic, spoken Algerian dialectal Arabic, Tamazight, French, and, recently emerging, English – pushed by the academic integration of the South, where French does not play a major role, as well as globally – Algeria might in the future capitalise on the opportunities offered by this encouraging environment. The politicisation of the language question reflects a contemporary identity conflict in society; Arab vis-à-vis African, Tamazight vis-à-vis Arab, and the tendency towards, as well as orientation to, France and Europe. Hence, Algeria is an illustration of African ambivalences (Macamo, 2005). This state of affairs reflects the oscillation and everyday contradictions.

Neither a comprehensive reform nor associated policies are likely to take place, or be implemented, without an empirical as well as conceptual reflection on the roles and functions of the Algerian university and its interactions with the members of the academic community, the general public, and the legislative, including, but by no means limited to, research. Furthermore, partners from the private sector and the diaspora do not (yet) partake in a strategic planning agenda with a clear-cut vision and mission. As evidenced by the data generated in this study, these activities will only be effective when carried out by social sciences, arts and humanities representatives, who should be acknowledged, encouraged, and supported in their on-going and future tasks at the service of society and thus the national common good.

On a micro level, there is the open question of individual responsibility and attitudes, in contrast to complaints about and blaming politics and the system, as frequently noted in the interviews. The mismanagement underlined may instead indicate individual competition, distrust, and lack of cooperation. In particular, those who possess motivation can succeed; after all, the diaspora is a product of the Algerian university, too. As for policy-induced system characterisation, the Algerian higher education system is currently undergoing a transition, which, however, is neither characterised by a transformation, nor the complete revitalisation observed in some sub-Saharan countries. Instead, the current development points towards a process of readjustment, the result of which may be labelled 'hybridisation'.

7.1 Higher Education Hybridisation: Attempt at Definition

Higher education hybridisation involves embracing, combining, and allowing for the co-existence of both local and global elements within a national higher education system, corresponding to respective policies. This approach implies retaining philosophies as nation-defining elements, derived from a country's history, culture, and religious values where applicable, while, at the same time, setting international standards for quality assurance in research and training. These standards should be applied by and within the academic community universally, and enable the framework conditions necessary, while acknowledging universities as complex and self-administering organisations and an integral component of knowledge societies, with institutional autonomy, individual mobility (both incoming and outgoing), and academic freedom, especially in the social sciences.

Hence, the resulting system is neither completely nationally nor internationally oriented, but is a hybrid. It does not reject and retreat from higher education internationalisation in its various forms, as a reaction to globalisation processes, yet it acknowledges the specific and unique political and social environment rather than succumbing to the illusion of objective, neutral institutions free from any parties' interest and ideology. Higher education hybridisation may be a characteristic of, and applicable to, transforming societies and welfare states. It is necessarily preceded by readjustment as a needs assessment in the form of the re-evaluation of international trends of higher education harmonisation not adapted to the local context, which is nowadays exemplified by the hasty, ill-considered adoption of the Bologna Process, locally as well as globally.

7.2   Application: Change Agent

Given the complexity of African and Arab contexts, particularly as transforming societies, and characterised by political, socioeconomic, cultural, and identity ambivalences[1], it is challenging and bureaucratically unwieldy to institutionalise quality assurance in the form of holistic higher education sector reforms. Not least, political will and considerable resources are a prerequisite. For this reason, it is deemed more suitable to respond to the hybrid situation on the macro and micro levels by individuals as a team of 'change agents' (Lunenburg, 2010; Nikolaou et al., 2007). These already exist in other sectors (Gerwing, 2016), or as agents of organisational development in non-governmental institutions (Battilana & Casciaro, 2012). In this way, an inexpensive interim solution is sought and implemented, while paving the way for systematic higher education transformation.

The process of higher education change management (Nordvall, 1982) and institutional development can be accompanied by those agents familiar with both the local context and international standards, either by their background as diaspora representatives, or as experts with bi/multicultural work experience and specific skills. Such agents can work within higher education institutions, and could include regulatory framework, human resources, ICT and quality assurance consultants; they could conceptualise and manage needs assessments and empirical studies; advise the government, other competent authorities, and institutional leadership on a strategic level; facilitate interaction with stakeholders outside the academic community; draft policy documents and national frameworks; conduct pilot projects as the first step of reform implementation; introduce and advise on knowledge and project management and communication

1   See Macamo, 2005.

structures; and build and sustain networks of actors (Schoelen et al., 2023).

Change agents also work as trainers and coaches for academic and administrative staff in higher education and governing authorities. In this way, they act as a bridge between the presently disconnected micro and macro levels by providing solutions, such as introducing and strengthening a meso level in the form of institutional autonomy in the case of Algeria. In doing so, change agents scale up hybrid coping strategies to manage academic ambivalences on the way to institutionalise strategies for facing global challenges as reflected by higher education internationalisation.

References

Ageron, C.-R. (1968). *Les algériens musulmans et la France (1871–1919)* (Tome 2). Presses Universitaires de France.

Ait Larbi, M. (2010). *Avril 1980*. Koukou.

Al Amin, A. (2016). Why the civil role of Arab universities ? (in Arabic): الافتتاحية: لماذا الدور المدني للجامعات العربية؟ *Lebanese Association for Educational Sciences*(36), 6–14 (Editorial).

Alexander, L. (2006). Academic Freedom. *University of Colorado Law Review*, 77(4), 883–900.

Algeria (1962). France-Algeria independence agreements (Evian agreements). *International Legal Materials*, 1(2), 214–230. https://www.jstor.org/stable/20689578

Almansour, S. (2016). The crisis of research and global recognition in Arab universities. *Near and Middle Eastern Journal of Research in Education*, 2016(1), 1. https://doi.org/10.5339/nmejre.2016.1

Altbach, P. G. (2001). Academic freedom: International realities and challenges. *Higher Education*, 41(1/2), 205–219. https://doi.org/10.1023/A:1026791518365

Altbach, P. G., Reisberg, L., Yudkevich, M., Androushchak, G., Kuzminov, & Yaroslav (Eds.). (2013). *The global future of higher education and the academic profession: The BRICs and the United States*. Palgrave Macmillan. https://books.google.de/books?id=7rGTW7F-B3kC https://doi.org/10.1057/9780230369795

Ambrose, C. M. (1990). Academic Freedom in American Public Colleges and Universities. *Review of Higher Education*, 14(1), 5–32.

Anderson, D., & Johnson, R. (1998). *University Autonomy in Twenty Countries*. Australian National University. http://www.magna-charta.org/resources/files/University_autonomy_in_20_countries.pdf

Andreescu, L. (2009). Foundations of Academic Freedom: Making New Sense of Some Aging Arguments. *Studies in Philosophy and Education*, 28(6), 499–515. https://doi.org/10.1007/s11217-009-9142-6

Arifi, A. (2016). The extent of Arab universities' commitment to community service: Evaluation of available university records (in Arabic): مدى التزام الجامعات العربية بخدمة المجتمع: تقييم سجلّات الجامعات المتاحة للجمهور *Lebanese Association for Educational Sciences*(36), 171–203.

Ashby, E. (1966a). Autonomy and Academic Freedom in Britain and in English-Speaking Countries of Tropical Africa. *Minerva*, 4(3), 317–364.

Ashby, E. (1966b). *Universities: British, Indian, African: A Study in the Ecology of Higher Education*. Harvard University Press.

Atkinson, R. C. (2004). Academic Freedom and the Research University. *Proceedings of the American Philosophical Society*, 148(2), 195–204. www.jstor.org/stable/1558284

Baddari, K., & Herzallah, A. (2014). *Référentiel LMD: Bien enseigner dans le système LMD*. OPU.

Baker, J. R. (1978). Michael Polanyi's Contributions to the Cause of Freedom in Science. *Minerva*, 13(3), 382–396. https://www.jstor.org/stable/pdf/41820340.pdf

Bakouche, S. (2011). Efficacité et efficience de l'enseignement supérieur en Algérie. In M. Ghalamallah (Ed.), *L'université algérienne et sa gouvernance* (pp. 151–165). CREAD.

Balandier, G. (1951). La situation coloniale: approche théorique. *Cahiers Internationaux De Sociologie*, 11, 44–79.

Barini, D. (2018). The role of the university in the development of the society (in Arabic). *Journal Afaq Al-Ulum*, 4, 164–174 (University Ziane Achour de Djelfa).

Battilana, J., & Casciaro, T. (2012). Change Agents, Networks, and Institutions: A Contingency Theory of Organizational Change. *Academy of Management Journal*, 55(2), 381–398. https://doi.org/10.5465/amj.2009.0891

Bauman, Z. (2013). *Modernity and Ambivalence*. Wiley.

Bayard, J.-F., & Bertrand, R. (2006). De quel 'legs colonial' parle-t-on? *Esprit* (Décembre), 134–160. https://esprit.presse.fr/article/bayart-jean-francois-et-bertrand-romain/de-quel-legs-colonial-parle-t-on-13808

Bedjaoui, M. (2018). *Une révolution algérienne à hauteur d'homme*. Préface de Jaques Frémeaux. Riveneuve.

Bellil, R. (1985). La domestication du savoir sur la société: remarques sur la sociologie en Algérie. *Annuaire De L'afrique Du Nord*, 505–535.

Benachenhou, M. (1980). *Vers l'Université Algérienne: Reflexions sur une Stratégie Universitaire*. Office des Publications universitaires (OPU).

Benleulmi, Z. & Hadiby-Ghoul, R. (2015). *Conduite du changement dans l'université algérienne. Objectif: Excellence*. Collection White Sea Business School.

Benaissa, A. (2017). Algeria's university in light of the economic transformations (in Arabic). *Annales De L'université D'alger*, 31(2), 173–192. https://www.asjp.cerist.dz/en/article/26546

Benghabrit, N., & Haddab, M. (Eds.). (2008). *L'Algérie 50 ans après. Etat des savoirs en sciences sociales et humaines 1954-2004*. Edition bilingue. Editions CRASC.

Bensouiah, A. (2018a, October 19). 'HE system under fire after political science is dropped'. *University World News*(229).

Bensouiah, A. (2018b, November 16). ALGERIA Unhappiness over postgraduate application process. *University World News*(231).

Bensouiah, A. (2019a, April 23). Universities at the heart of anti-government protests. *University World News*. https://www.universityworldnews.com/post.php?story=20190423145313877

Bensouiah, A. (2019b, September 28). Arab Universities to have their own Classification System. *University World News*. https://www.universityworldnews.com/post.php?story=20190926090253994

Bensouiah, A. (2020a, January 21). New minister puts damper on switch to English in HE. *University World News*. https://www.universityworldnews.com/post.php?story=20200121075558324

Bensouiah, A. (2020b, January 30). University academics prepare demands for new minister. *University World News*. https://www.universityworldnews.com/post.php?story=20200129070232361

Bensouiah, A. (2020c, February 12). President's Twitter appeal fails to stem student protest. *University World News*. https://www.universityworldnews.com/post.php?story=20200212063345661

Bensouiah, A. (2020d, February 27). Minister seeks ways to boost ethics, reduce plagiarism. *University World News*. https://www.universityworldnews.com/post.php?story=20200226120220451

Benstaali, B. (2019). Higher Education Partnership between Maghreb and European Higher Education Institutions during the 2002–2013 Decade. In C. Scherer & E. T. Woldegiorgis (Eds.), *African higher education: developments and perspectives: Volume 4. Partnership in Higher Education: Trends Between African and European Institutions* (pp. 103–119). Brill Sense. https://doi.org/10.1163/9789004411876_006

Bettahar, Y. (2008). Les Sources de l'enseignement supérieur colonial au Centre des archives d'outre-mer et au Centre des archives nationales d'Algérie. In M.-J. Choffel-Mailfert & L. Rollet (Eds.), *Mémoire et culture matérielle de l'université. Sauvegarde, valorisation et recherche* (pp. 63–77). Presses Univ. de Nancy.

Bettahar, Y. (2014). L'Université d'Alger: une transposition singulière de l'université républicaine en terre algérienne (XIXe-XX siècles). In Y. Bettahar & M.-J. Choffel-Mailfert (Eds.), *Collection 'Histoire des institutions scientifiques'. Les universités au risque de l'histoire: Principes, configurations, modèles* (pp. 115–154). Presses universitaires de Nancy; Éditions universitaires de Lorraine.

Birley, R. (1972). *The Real Meaning of Academic Freedom.* World University Service (WUS).

Bloland, H. (1969). *The Politicization of Higher Education Organizations: Assets and Liabilities.* https://files.eric.ed.gov/fulltext/ED027850.pdf

Bouab, R. (2016). The educational and social function of the University professor in the LMD system (French Abstract). *Journal of Human and Social Science (28)* 21, 213-236.

Boukhobza, M. (1991). *Octobre 1988. Evolution ou rupture ?* Edition Bouchene.

Boumediene, M., & Beddi, N. (2015). De l'innovation à la croissance: au rythme du dynamisme de l'enseignement supérieur. *Revue Algérienne De Finances Publiques*, 5, 31–61.

Bourdieu, P. (1986). The forms of capital. In J. G. Richardson (Ed.), *Handbook of theory and research for the sociology of education* (15–29 (241-258)). Greenwood Press. http://www.socialcapitalgateway.org/sites/socialcapitalgateway.org/files/data/paper/2016/10/18/rbasicsbourdieu1986-theformsofcapital.pdf

Brown, E. E. (1900). Academic Freedom. *Educational Review*, 19(3), 209–231.

Castells, M. (1993). The university system: Engine of development in the new world economy. In A. Ransom (Ed.), *EDI seminar series. Improving higher education in developing countries* (pp. 65–80). World Bank.

Castells, M. (2001). Universities as dynamic systems of contradictory functions. In M. Castells, J. Müller, N. Cloete, & S. Timol-Badat (Eds.), *Higher education and globalisation: Vol. 4. Challenges of globalisation: South African debates with Manuel Castells* (pp. 206–223). Maskew Miller Longman.

Chachoua, K. (2015). Les révoltes au pays de la Révolution. Champ intellectuel, champ du pouvoir et 'révoltes arabes' en Algérie. *Revue Des Mondes Musulmans Et De La Méditerranée, 2015.2*(138), 189–206.

Chachoua, K. (2018). Un délire bien fondé. *Revue Des Mondes Musulmans Et De La Méditerranée*(144), 45–60.

Cherif, M. (2013). *Le défi du savoir en Algérie: Réflexions.* ANEP.

Colonna, F. (1972). Le système d'enseignement de l'Algérie coloniale. *European Journal of Sociology / Archives Européennes De Sociologie / Europäisches Archiv Für Soziologie, 13*(2), 195–220. www.jstor.org/stable/23998582

Colonna, F. (1975). *Instituteurs algériens: 1883-1939. Travaux et recherches de science politique: Vol. 36.* Pr. de la Fondation Nationale des Sciences Polit.

Colonna, F. (2008). Training the National Elites in Colonial Algeria 1920-1954. *Historical Social Research/Historische Sozialforschung, 33*(2 (124)), 285–295. www.jstor.org/stable/20762288

Daghbouche, N. *Status and socio-professional problems of Algerian universities.*

Daghbouche, N. (1982). *Higher Education in Algeria - strategical problems* [Magister]. University of Cardiff, Cardiff. http://www.ccdz.cerist.dz/admin/bib_loc.php?id=0000000000000238044000000

Daghbouche, N. (2008). A Systematic Approach: A Solution to Algerian Higher Education. *Forum De L'enseignant, 4*(Avril), 72–85.

Daghbouche, N. (2011). The impact of the credit transfer accumulation system on Algeria. *The Journal of North African Studies, 16*(3), 465–470.

Dahmane, M. (2014). *Les fondements des systèmes nationaux d'information scientifique et technique: Cas de l'Algérie.* Office des Publications universitaires (OPU).

Derguini, A. (2011). Gouvernance des universités. De la massification à la diversification, transformer une faiblesse en une force. In M. Ghalamallah (Ed.), *L'université algérienne et sa gouvernance* (pp. 101–131). CREAD.

Direction Générale de la Recherche Scientifique et du Développement Technologique. (2015). *L'Evolution de la Recherche Scientifique dans le Monde et en Algérie de 2000 à 2014.* DGRSDT.

Direction Générale de la Recherche Scientifique et du Développement Technologique. (2019a). *Document préliminaire Stratégie Nationale de la Recherche Sectorielle Horizon 2015: Vision et Plan d'action.* DGRSDT.

Direction Générale de la Recherche Scientifique et du Développement Technologique. (2019b). *Etat des Lieux du Potentiel Scientifique dans les Etablissements du MESRS-Algérie.* DGRDST.

Direction Générale de la Recherche Scientifique et du Développement Technologique. (2019c). *Production Scientifique en Algérie: Juin 2019.* DGRSDT.

Direction Générale de la Recherche Scientifique et du Développement Technologique. (2020). *Census of National Scientific Journals (Updated 05/03/2020).*

Djeflat, A. (1990). Développement économique et développement universitaire: complémentarité et enjeux à la lumière de l'expérience algérienne. *Revue Tunisienne De Sciences Sociales, 27ème annee*(100), 35–55.

Dresing, T., & Pehl, T. (2015). *Manual (on) Transcription: Transcription Conventions, Software Guides and Practical Hints for Qualitative Researchers* (3. Engl. Ed., January 2015). dr. dresing et pehl GmbH. https://www.audiotranskription.de/download/manual_on_transcription.pdf

Drif, Z. (2013). *Mémoires d'une combattante de l'ALN, zone autonome d'Alger*. Edition Chihab.

E.B. (2001). Hilaliens. In G. Camps (Ed.), *Encyclopédie berbère* (Vol. 23). ÉDISUD. https://journals.openedition.org/encyclopedieberbere/1593

Estermann, T., Nokkala, T., & Steinel, M. (2011). *University autonomy in Europe II: The scorecard.* European University Association (EUA). https://eua.eu/downloads/publications/university%20autonomy%20in%20europe%20ii%20-%20the%20scorecard.pdf

Faruqi, Y. M. (2006). Contributions of Islamic scholars to the scientific enterprise. *International Education Journal*, 7(4), 391–399.

Garcés, M. A. (2005). *Cervantes in Algiers: A captive's tale* (1. paperback ed.).

Germany Trade and Invest. (May 2020). *Wirtschaftsdaten kompakt Algerien.* Germany Trade and Invest (GTAI). https://www.gtai.de/resource/blob/14974/eaa6bed7b169bc2dbaf0031473555a51/gtai-wirtschaftsdaten-mai-2020-algerien-data.pdf

Gerwing, C. (2016). Meaning of Change Agents within Organisational Change. *Journal of Applied Leadership and Management*, 4, 21–40. http://www.journal-alm.org/article/view/17107

Ghalamallah, M. *Elements de réflexion sur l'Université, sa vocation et ses fonctions.* Unité de Recherche en Anthropologie Sociale et Culturelle (U.R.A.S.C.).

Ghalamallah, M. (2006). L'Université algérienne: Genèse des contraintes structurelles, conditions par une mise à niveau. *Les Cahiers Du CREAD*, 77, 31–52 (Etude sur l'Université algérienne).

Ghalamallah, M. (Ed.). (2011a). *L'université algérienne et sa gouvernance.* CREAD.

Ghalamallah, M. (2011b). Université, savoir et société en Algérie. In M. Ghalamallah (Ed.), *L'université algérienne et sa gouvernance* (pp. 15–55). CREAD.

Ghanmy, M. (2018, August 10). Row over Algerian education minister's Nobel Prize comments. *Al Arabiya.Net.* https://english.alarabiya.net/en/News/north-africa/2018/08/10/Algerian-minister-s-says-Nobel-Prize-won-t-add-to-education-sparks-anger

Gläser, J., & Laudel, G. (2010). *Experteninterviews und qualitative Inhaltsanalyse als Instrumente rekonstruierender Untersuchungen* (4. Auflage). *Lehrbuch.* VS Verlag. http://d-nb.info/1002141753/04

Gläser, J., & Laudel, G. (2016). On Interviewing 'Good' and 'Bad' Experts. In A. Bogner (Ed.), *Interviewing Experts* (pp. 117-137). Palgrave Macmillan.

Glasman, D., & Kremer, J. (1978). *Essai sur l'Université et les cadres en Algérie: Une technocratie sans technologie ? Les Cahiers du C.R.E.S.M: Vol. 8.* Centre de Recherche et d'Etudes sur les Sociétés Méditerranéennes (CRESM).

Guerid, D. (2007). *L'exception algérienne. La Modernisation à l'épreuve de la société.* Casbah.

Guerid, D. (2010, January 6). L'Université algérienne a 100 ans. *Le Quotidien D'Oran*, pp. 9–10.

Guerid, D. (2012a). L'Université dans la société du savoir. In D. Guerid (Ed.), *Savoir et société en Algérie* (pp. 21–43). Centre Recherche en Economic Appliquee pour le Developpment.

Guerid, D. (2012b). Présentation: Savoirs explicites et savoirs implicites. In D. Guerid (Ed.), *Savoir et société en Algérie* (pp. 5–19). Centre Recherche en Economic Appliquee pour le Developpment.

Gutmann, A. (1983). Is Freedom Indivisible ? The Relative Autonomy of Universities in a Liberal Democracy. In J. R. Pennock & J. W. Chapman (Eds.), *(Nomos: 25). Liberal democracy* (pp. 257–286). Univ. Pr.

Habart, M. (2013). Histoire d'un parjure. In A. Sekfali (Ed.), *L'histoire illustree et commentee de la medersat El hayet-Jijel, 1933-1962* (pp. 137–139). Dār al-Almaʻīyah lil-Nashr wa-al-Tawzīʻ.

Haddab, M. (2014). *Dimensions du champ* éducatif *algérien: Analyses et* évaluations. Arak éditions.

Hamet, I. (1932). Notice sur les Arabes hilaliens. *Revue D'historie Des Colonies*, 20(87), 241–264. https://www.persee.fr/docAsPDF/outre_0399-1385_1932_num_20_87_2836.pdf

Hanafi, S. (2011). University systems in the Arab East: Publish globally and perish locally vs publish locally and perish globally. *Current Sociology*, 59(3), 291–309. https://doi.org/10.1177/0011392111400782

Haroun, A. (2014). *Le Rempart*. Casbah.

Hayesh, M., & Boubaker, H. (2016). The value function of the university in achieving the dimensions of national unity (in Arabic): الوظيفة القيمية للجامعة في تحقيق أبعاد الوحدة الوطنية. *MAAREF*, 11(20), 162–180.

Heggoy, A. A. (1973). Education in French Algeria: An Essay on Cultural Conflict. *Comparative Education Review*, 17(2), 180–197. www.jstor.org/stable/1186812

Heisler, M. O. (2007). Academic Freedom and the Freedom of Academics: Toward a Transnational Civil Society Move. *International Studies Perspectives*, 8(4), 347–357. http://www.jstor.com/stable/44218512

Iqbal, A. (1972). Karl Jasper's Idea of Academic Freedom. *Intellect*, *101*(95-6), 23–44.

James, G. G. M. (1992). *Stolen legacy* (1st Africa World Press ed.). Africa World Press, Inc.

Kadri, A. (1991). De l'université coloniale à l'université nationale: Instrumentalisation et 'idéologisation' de l'institution. *Peuples Méditerranéens*, *54-55*, 151–184 (Sciences Sociales Sociétés Arabes).

Kadri, A. (2000). La formation à l'étranger des étudiants algériens : limites d'une politique (1962-1995). In V. Geisser (Ed.), *Diplômés maghrébins d'ici et d'ailleurs. Trajectoires sociales et itinéraires migratoires* (pp. 209–219). CNRS.

Kadri, A. (2007). Histoire du système d'enseignement colonial en Algérie. In F. Abécassis, G. Boyer, B. Falaize, G. Meynier, & M. Zancarini-Fournel (Eds.), *La France et l'Algérie : leçons d'histoire* (pp. 19–39). ENS Éditions. https://doi.org/10.4000/books.enseditions.1268

Kadri, A., & Ghouati, A. (2006). *Enseignants et instituteurs en Algérie:Les luttes enseignantes dans la décolonisation 1945-1965*. Unsa Education. https://hal.archives-ouvertes.fr/hal-01341823/document

Karran, T. (2007). Academic Freedom in Europe: A Preliminary Comparative Analysis. *Higher Education Policy*, *20*(3), 289–313. https://doi.org/10.1057/palgrave.hep.8300159

Karran, T. (2009). Academic Freedom in Europe: Time for a Magna Charta? *Higher Education Policy*, *22*(2), 163–189. https://doi.org/10.1057/hep.2009.2

Kateb, K. (2014). *Le système éducatif dans l'Algérie coloniale: 1833-1962 : bilan statistique historiographique*. APIC.

Khader, F. (2009). *Strategies and Roadmap for Effective Higher Education in Jordan*. University of Petra. https://www.uop.edu.jo/download/research/members/111_1548_khad.pdf

Khelfaoui, H. (1996). Conditions d'émergence d'une communauté scientifique en Algérie: savoirs et pouvoirs de 1962 à 1992. *Cahiers Des Sciences Humaines*, 3(32). http://horizon. documentation.ird.fr/exl-doc/pleins_textes/pleins_ textes_4/sci_hum/010008302.pdf

Khelfaoui, H. (2000). Savoir, savoir diplômé et répresentations sociales en Algérie (1962-1998). In V. Geisser (Ed.), *Diplômés maghrébins d'ici et d'ailleurs. Trajectoires sociales et itinéraires migratoires* (pp. 56–65). CNRS.

Khelfaoui, H. (2003). Le champ universitaire algérien entre pouvoirs politiques et champ économique. *Actes De La Recherche En Sciences Sociales*, 148(3), 34. https://doi. org/10.3917/arss.148.0034

Khelfaoui, H. (2004). Scientific Research in Algeria Institutionalisation versus Professionalisation. Science, Technology and Society, 9(1), 75–101. https://doi. org/10.1177/097172180400900104

Khelfaoui, H. (2010). Algérie: le rapport savoir-pouvoir ou le rêveavorté de la différenciation par le savoir. Journal of Higher Education in Africa/Revue De L'enseignement Supérieur En Afrique, 8(2), 23–38.

Khelfaoui, H. (2012). Higher Education and Differentiation on Knowledge: Algeria's Aborted Dream. In A. E. Mazawi & R. G. Sultana (Eds.), World Yearbook of Education. World Yearbook of Education 2010: Education and the Arab 'World': Political Projects, Struggles, and Geometries of Power (pp. 273–284). Taylor and Francis.

Khelfaoui, H., & Ogachi, I. O. (2011). Introduction: Academic Freedom in Africa: Between local powers and international donors. Journal of Higher Education in Africa/Revue De L'enseignement Supérieur En Afrique, 9(1 &2), v–xiii. http://awdflibrary. org/bitstream/handle/123456789/459/en-2. pdf?sequence=1&isAllowed=y

Kirk, R. (1955, 1977). *Academic freedom: An essay in definition.* Greenwood Press.

Kuhn, J. C., & Aby, S. H. (2000). Academic freedom: A guide to the literature. Bibliographies and indexes in education: no. 20. Greenwood Press. https://books.google.de/books?id=ItoS0uwUsCsC

Ladjal, T., & Bensaid, B. (2014). A Cultural Analysis of Ottoman Algeria (1516 - 1830): The North–South Mediterranean Progress Gap. Islam and Civilisational Renewal, 5(4), 567–585. https://doi.org/10.12816/0009884

Langa, P. V. (2010). Disciplines and engagement in African universities : A study of the distribution of scientific capital and academic networking in social sciences [Dissertation, University of Cape Town, Cape Town]. open.uct.ac.za. https://open.uct.ac.za/bitstream/11427/14621/1/thesis_hum_2010_langa_patra_shy_cio_vitorino.pdf

Langa, P. V. (2011). The significance of Bourdieu's cultural capital in analysing the field of higher education in Mozambique. International Journal of Contemporary Sociology, 48(1), 93–116.

Lardjane, O. (Ed.). (2007). Elite et société, Algérie & Egypte. Casbah.

Laskaris, E. (2016). La coopération culturelle franco-algérienne. Les coopérants français en Algérie indépendante. Enseignants des écoles (instituteurs et professeurs) et universitaires (1962-1980) [Thesis]. Université Paris-Est, Paris. https://tel.archives-ouvertes.fr/tel-01691333/document

Leslie, D. W. (1986). Academic Freedom for Universities. *The Review of Higher Education*, 9(2), 135–157. https://doi.org/10.1353/rhe.1986.0028

Lunenburg, F. C. (2010). Managing Change: The Role of the Change Agent. *International Journal of Management, Business, and Administration*, 13(1), 1–6.

Lüscher, K. (2011a). Ambivalence: A 'Sensitizing Construct' for the Study and Practice of Intergenerational Relationships. *Journal of Intergenerational Relationships*(9), 191–206.

Lüscher, K. (2011b). Ambivalenz weiterschreiben: Eine wissenssoziologisch-pragmatische Perspektive. *Forum Psychoanalyse*, 27, 373–393. http://kurtluescher.de/downloads/KL_Ambivalenz_weiterschreiben.pdf

Macamo, E. (Ed.). (2005). *Africa in the New Millennium. Negotiating modernity: Africa's ambivalent experience.* Codesria Books; Zed Books; University of South Africa Press. http://www.loc.gov/catdir/enhancements/fy0665/2005043321-b.html

Mahiou, A. (2013). La réforme de l'enseignement supérieur en Algérie. Libres propos d'un acteur. In J.-R. Henry & J.-C. Vatin (Eds.), Le temps de la coopération. Sciences Sociales et décolonisation au Maghreb (pp. 297–320). Karthala.

Mahiou, A. (2015). La réforme de l'enseignement supérieur en Algérie: quelques souvenirs personnels. Revue Algérienne Des Sciences Juridiques, Economiques Et Politiques, 52(3), 5–33.

Mammeri, M. (1989). Une expérience de recherche anthropologique en Algérie. AWAL(5), 15–23 [traduit vers l'arabe par Fella Bendjilali and Kamel Chachoua Alger, CNRPAH, 2015].).

Mayring, P. (2015). Qualitative Content Analysis: Theoretical Foundation, Basic Procedures and Software Solution. https://www.ssoar.info/ssoar/bitstream/handle/document/39517/ssoar-2014-mayring-Qualitative_content_analysis_theoretical_foundation.pdf?sequence=1&isAllowed=y&lnkname=ssoar-2014-mayring-Qualitative_content_analysis_theoretical_foundation.pdf

Mazawi, A. E., & Sultana, R. G. (2012). Editorial Introduction: Situating the 'Worlds' of Arab Education. In A. E. Mazawi & R. G. Sultana (Eds.), World Yearbook of Education. World Yearbook of Education 2010: Education and the Arab 'World': Political Projects, Struggles, and Geometries of Power (pp. 1–40). Taylor and Francis.

Mazrui, M. A. (1975). Academic Freedom in Africa: The Dual Tyranny. African Affairs, 75(297), 393–400.

McDaniel, O. C. (1996). The paradigms of governance in higher education systems. Higher Education Policy, 9(2), 137–158. https://doi.org/10.1016/S0952-8733(96)00005-0

McGucken, W. (1978). On freedom and planning in science: The Society for Freedom in Science, 1940?46. *Minerva*, *16*(1), 42–72. https://doi.org/10.1007/BF01102181

Mediterranean Network of National Information Centres on the Recognition of Qualifications. (2019). *The Higher Education system in Algeria: National Report.* MERIC-Net.

Mélia, J. (1950). L'Epopée Intellectuelle de l'Algérie: Histoire de l'Université d'Alger. La Maison des Livres.

Merrouche, O. (2007). The Long Term Impact of French Settlement on Education in Algeria (Department of Economics Working Paper No. 2). Uppsala University.

Merzouk, M. (2012). Les nouvelles formes de religiosité juvénile: enquête en milieu étudiant. Insaniyat - Revue Algérienne D'anthropologie Et De Sciences Sociales, 16(55-56), 121–131.

Meuser, M. & Nagel, U. (2002). ExpertInneninterviews - vielfach erprobt, wenig bedacht. In A. Bogner, B. Littig & W. Menz. (Eds), Das Experteninterview (pp. 71–93). VS Verlag für Sozialwissenschaften.

Meynier, G. (2007). L'Algérie des origines: De la préhistoire à l'avènement de l'islam. La Découverte.

Meynier, G. (2014). L'Algérie et les Algériens sous le système colonial. Approche historico historiographique. *Insaniyat /إنسانيات*(65–66), 13–70. https://doi.org/10.4000/insaniyat.14758

Miliani, M. & Sebaa, R. (2021). *L'université post-reforme en Algérie.* CRASC.

Ministère de l'Enseignement Supérieur et de la Recherche Scientifique. (1971). *La Refonte de l'Enseignement Supérieur. Principes et régime des études des nouveaux diplômes universitaires.* Ministère de l'Enseignement Supérieur et la Recherche Scientifique (MESRS)L.

Ministère de l'Enseignement Supérieur et de la Recherche Scientifique. (2019). *Textes législatifs et réglementaires du secteur de l'enseignement supérieur et de la recherche scientifique, 2005-2019.* https://www.mesrs.dz/documents/12221/32648/Textes-Reglementaires-Fr-2005-2016.pdf/75f41cc6-2472-4ce1-b5fd-aa8287659ef6

Ministère de l'Enseignement Supérieur et de la Recherche Scientifique. (2020a). *CHAPITRE I: Accords de coopération dans le domaine de l'enseignement supérieur et de la recherche scientifique.* https://www.mesrs.dz/fr/chapitre1

Ministère de l'Enseignement Supérieur et de la Recherche Scientifique. (2020b). *Communiqué de Presse Alger le 20 Janvier 2020: Le Pr. Chems-Eddine CHITOUR a procédé au lancement,par visio conférence,destravauxde la réunion du Conseil National d'Éthique et de Déontologie tenue aujourd'hui (20 Janvier 2020) à l'Université de Bechar - TAHRI Mohammed.*

Ministère de l'Enseignement Supérieur et de la Recherche Scientifique. (2020c). *Communiqué de Presse Alger, le 27 Février 2020: Le Pr. Chitour préside les travaux d'une rencontre de concertation avec les chefs des* établissements *universitaireset responsables pédagogiques.* MESRS. https://www.mesrs.dz/documents/21525/80662/%232+Communiqu%C3%A9+de+Presse+Alger+le+27+f%C3%A9vrier+2020-FR.pdf/07e4ff8b-6272-455d-b393-b95b5b11a744

Ministère de l'Enseignement Supérieur et de la Recherche Scientifique. (2020d, January 5). *Le Pr. Chems-Eddine Chitour prend ses fonctions à la tête du Ministère de l'Enseignement Supérieur.* https://www.mesrs.dz/activite/-/asset_publisher/ylWq1hBeIHRB/content/--9-21?inheritRedirect=false&redirect=https%3A%2F%2Fwww.mesrs.dz%2Factivite%3Fp_p_id%3D101_INSTANCE_ylWq1hBeIHRB%26p_p_lifecycle%3D0%26p_p_state%3Dnormal%26p_p_mode%3Dview%26p_p_col_id%3Dcolumn-1%26p_p_col_pos%3D2%26p_p_col_count%3D3

Ministère de l'Enseignement Supérieur et de la Recherche Scientifique. (2013). *L'Enseignement Supérieur et la Recherche Scientifique en Algérie: 50 Années au service du développement 1962-2012.* Office des Publications universitaires (OPU), pp. 19–124.

Ministère de l'Education Nationale. Sécretariat Général Service de la Planification et de la Carte Scolaire. (1966). *Guide de l'enseignement supérieur en Algérie.* Supplement N. 2 de la Publication mensuelle 'Informations et Documents'. Ministère de l'Education Nationale.

Ministère des Finances. (2018). *Rapport de Présentation du Projet de la Loi de Finances pour 2018 et Prévisions 2019-2020.* http://www.dgpp-mf.gov.dz/images/stories/PDF/RPLF/aplf2018.pdf

Mortimer, R. A. (1970). The Algerian Revolution in Search of the African Revolution. *The Journal of Modern African Studies,* *8*(3), 363–387. www.jstor.org/stable/158849

Mortimer, R. A. (2015). Algerian foreign policy: from revolution to national interest. *The Journal of North African Studies*, 20(3), 466–482. https://doi.org/10.1080/13629387.2014. 990961

Natter, K. (2014). *Fifty years of Maghreb emigration: How states shaped Algerian, Moroccan and Tunisian emigration.* Working Papers (No. 95). https://www.migrationinstitute. org/files/events/natter-1.pdf

Natter, K. (2020). *Maghreb – Migration Patterns and Policies between the Sahara and the Mediterranean: The growth and distribution of Maghreb emigrant populations, 1960 – 2017* [Regional Profile North Africa]. Bundeszentrale für politische Bildung (BpB). https://m.bpb.de/gesellschaft/ migration/laenderprofile/304866/morocco-algeria-and-tunisia

Ncube, P. (Ed.). (2010). *Quality higher education in SADC: Challenges and opportunities : proceedings of the first Higher Education Quality Management Initiative for Southern Africa (HEQMISA) International Conference, Benoni, South Africa, 24-26 November 2009.* UVW, UniversitätsVerlagWebler.

Ndiaye, A. L. (1996). The Case of Francophone Africa. *Higher Education Policy*, 9(4), 299–302. https://doi.org/10.1016/ S0952-8733(96)00026-8

Nikolaou, I., Gouras, A., Vakola, M., & Bourantas, D. (2007). Selecting Change Agents: Exploring Traits and Skills in a Simulated Environment. *Journal of Change Management*, 7(3-4), 291–313. https://doi. org/10.1080/14697010701779173

Nordvall, R. C. (1982). *The Process of Change in Higher Education Institutions.* AAHE-ERIC/Higher Education Research Report (No. 7).

O'Leary, Z. (2017). *The Essential Guide to Doing your Research Project.* SAGE.

Organisation of Economic Cooperation and Development (OECD). (2020). *OECD Education Statistics (Database): Education at a glance: Educational attainment and labour-force status*. OECD. https://doi.org/10.1787/889e8641-en

Pervillé, G. (2004). *Les* étudiants *algériens de l'Université française, 1880 - 1962: Populisme et nationalisme chez les* étudiants *et intellectuels musulmans algériens de formation française. Collection 'Histoire de l'Algérie contemporaine'*. Casbah Éd.

Polanyi, M., Ziman, J., & Fuller, S. (2000). The Republic of Science: Its political and economic theory, I(1) (1962), 54-73. *Minerva, 38*(1), 1–32. www.jstor.org/stable/41821153

Rauschmayer, B., Rosenbusch, C., Wollny, C., & Schmidt, U. (2010). An empirical study on quality management practices and structures at higher education institutions in SADC : survey results on institutional quality assurance in SADC. In P. Ncube (Ed.), *Quality higher education in SADC: Challenges and opportunities : proceedings of the first Higher Education Quality Management Initiative for Southern Africa (HEQMISA) International Conference, Benoni, South Africa, 24-26 November 2009.* UVW, UniversitätsVerlagWebler.

Remaoun, H. (Ed.). (2000). *L'Algérie: histoire, société et culture.* Casbah. https://scholar.google.com/citations?user=pbllyloaaaaj&hl=en&oi=sra

République Française. (1960). *Université d'Alger: Cinquantenaire 1909-1959.* Imprimerie Officielle de le Délégation Générale du Gouvernement en Algérie.

Ridwan, B. (2015). The functional and social functioning of the University professor in the new (LMD) system (in Arabic). *University Mohamed Seddik Ben Yahia Jijel,* (21), 71-86.

Ronze, R. (1930). *L'Algérie du Centenaire vue par l'Université de France.* Publications du Comité national métropolitain du centenaire de l'Algérie.

Rouighi, R. (2019a). *Inventing the Berbers: History and ideology in the Maghrib. The Middle Ages series.* University of Pennsylvania Press.

Rouighi, R. (2019b, September 18). Race on the mind. *Aeon.*

Russell, C., & Russell, W. M. S. (1999). *Population crises and population cycles.* The Galton Institute.

Sabour, M. (1988). Homo Academicus Arabicus. *Publications in Social Sciences*, 11.

Sabour, M. (2001). *The ontology and status of intellectuals in Arab academia and society.* Ashgate.

Saldaña, J. (2016). *The coding manual for qualitative researchers.* SAGE. 3rd edition.

Schmidt, U. (2007). Requirements for a system of internal quality assurance in higher education institutions. In B. Michalk (Ed.), *Beiträge zur Hochschulpolitik: Vol. 2007,13. The quality assurance system for higher education at European and national level: Bologna Seminar, Berlin, 15 and 16 February 2007 ; [Bologna-Seminar The Quality Assurance System for Higher Education at European and National Level ; diese Publikation ist im Rahmen des Projektes Qualitätsmanagement entstanden* (pp. 112–121). Hochschulrektorenkonferenz.

Scholars at Risk. (2020). *Who is considered a 'Scholar at Risk' ? FAQs.* SAR. https://www.scholarsatrisk.org/faqs/

Schoelen, L. (2023). Between National Identity, Research and Social Function. Academics' Perceptions of the Ambivalent Role of the Algerian University. In B.K. Daniel & R. Bisaso (Eds.), *Higher Education in Sub-Saharan Africa in the 21st Century* (pp. 221-233). Springer.

Singaravélou, P. (2009). L'enseignement supérieur colonial. Un état des lieux. *Histoire de l'éducation*(122), 71–92. https://doi.org/10.4000/histoire-education.1942

Soyer, M., & Gilbert, P. (2012). Debating on the origins of sociology: Ibn Khaldun as a founding father of sociology. *International Journal of Sociological Research*, 5(1-2), 13–30.

Staïfi, M. (2013, October 2). Dans le fief des SHS (sciences humaines et sociales): Alger III Bouzareah. *El Watan*.

Sutherland, E. (2020). The Fourth Industrial Revolution – The Case of South Africa. *Politikon*, 47(2), 233–252. https://doi.org/10.1080/02589346.2019.1696003

Times Higher Education (THE) World Universities Ranking. (2019). *Top Universities in Algeria*. https://www.timeshighereducation.com/student/where-to-study/study-in-algeria

Turin, Y. (1971). *Affrontements culturels dans l'Algérie coloniale. Ecoles, médecine, religion, 1830-1880*. Editions Maspéro.

UNESCO, & Varghese, N. V. (2013). *Governance reforms and university autonomy in Asia* (IIEP Research Papers). United Nations Educational, Scientific and Cultural Organisation (UNESCO). http://euniam.aau.dk/fileadmin/user_upload/Varghese____Martin_2013_Gov_reforms-Univ_autonomy_Asia.pdf

UNESCO, & Varghese, N. V. (2016). *Governance reforms in higher education: A study of selected countries in Africa* (IIEP Research Papers). United Nations Educational, Scientific and Cultural Organisation (UNESCO). https://unesdoc.unesco.org/ark:/48223/pf0000245404

United Nations Development Programme (UNDP). (2019). *Human Development Report 2019 Inequalities in Human Development in the 21st Century: Briefing note for countries on the 2019 Human Development Report Algeria*. http://hdr.undp.org/sites/all/themes/hdr_theme/country-notes/DZA.pdf

Schoelen, L., Sebihi, A., Azab-Els, S. et al. (2023). Diversity of epistemologies in African higher education: an interdisciplinary perspective on the contribution of digital communities of practice to equitable knowledge production. *Curriculum Perspectives 43* (Suppl 1). 117–125. https://doi.org/10.1007/s41297-023-00209-8

Schreier, M. (2013). *Qualitative content analysis in practice.* SAGE.

Schreier, M. (2014). Varianten qualitativer Inhaltsanalyse: Ein Wegweiser im Dickicht der Begrifflichkeiten. *Forum Qualitative Sozialforschung / Forum: Qualitative Social Research*, 15 (1). 10.17169/fqs-15.1.2043.

Sebihi, A., & Schoelen, L. (2019). Developing International Quality Assurance Standards in Africa: Reference to the Pan-African University as Institutional Partnership in the Framework of Bologna. In E. T. Woldegiorgis & C. Scherer (Eds.), *African higher education: developments and perspectives: Volume 4. Partnership in Higher Education: Trends Between African and European Institutions* (pp. 120–137). Brill Sense.

Sebihi, A. & Schoelen, L. (2020). Linguistic Coexistence and Controversy in Algerian Higher Education. From Colonialisation via the Arabisation Movement to the Adoption of Hybridity. In I. Turner, E.T Woldegiorgis & A. Brahima (Eds.), *Indigenous Knowledge and Decolonization in African Higher Education* (Chapter 7, pp. 140-158). Routledge Taylor & Francis.

Shirley, R. C. (1984). Institutional Autonomy and Governmental Control. *The Educational Forum*, 48(2), 217–222. https://doi.org/10.1080/00131728409335897

Sidi Boumediene, R. (2013). *Yaoueled, parcours d'un indigène.*

Siino, F. (2014). Malentendus dans la décolonisation. Coopérants de l'enseignement supérieur au Maghreb (1960-1980). In S. El Machat & F. Renucci (Eds.), *Racines du présent. Les Décolonisations au XXe siècle: Les hommes de la transition: itinéraires, actions et traces* (pp. 247–286). L'Harmattan.

United Nations Educational, Scientific and Cultural Organisation. (2020). *Algeria. Education and Literacy.* UNESCO. http://uis.unesco.org/en/country/dz?theme=education-and-literacy

United Nations Educational, Scientific and Cultural Organisation (UNESCO)/ Institute for Statistics. (2020a). *Education: Gross enrolment ratio by level of education.* UNESCO. http://data.uis.unesco.org/index.aspx?queryid=142

United Nations Educational, Scientific and Cultural Organisation (UNESCO)/Institute for Statistics. (2020b). *Algeria. Science, Technology and Innovation.* UNESCO. http://uis.unesco.org/en/country/dz?theme=science-technology-and-innovation

United Nations University. (2009). Revitalising higher education in Sub-Saharan Africa: A United Nations University Project Report. United Nations University (UNU).

University World News (2019, December 4). Vast majority of Arab researchers would rather emigrate. *University World News.* https://www.universityworldnews.com/post.php?story=20191204084049150

University World News/Algérie Press Service (2018, November 16). ALGERIA 72 laboratories shut after 'negative assessments'. University World News(231). https://bit.ly/47j9eii

University World News/Algérie Press Service (2019, November 14). African Union sets up commission for Tamazight language. University World News. https://www.universityworldnews.com/post.php?story=20191111081745330

Wallon, D. (2014). Combats étudiants pour l'independance de l'Algérie: UNEF–UGEMA (1955–1962). Collection essais. Casbah Éditions.

Williams, R. L. (2006). Academic Freedom in Higher Education Within a Conservative Sociopolitical Culture. Innovative Higher Education, 31(1), 5–25. https://doi.org/10.1007/s10755-006-9005-9

Wilson, B. (1997). Politicizing Academic Freedom, Vulgarizing Scholarly Discourse. Chronicle of Higher Education, 44(17), A52.

Yeo, A., Legard, R., Keegan, J., Ward, K., McNaughton Nicholls, K., & Lewis, J. (2014). In-depth Interviews. In J. Ritchie (Ed.), Qualitative research practice: A guide for social science students and researchers (2nd edition, pp. 177–210). SAGE.

Zavale, N. C., & Langa, P. V. (2018). African Diaspora and the Search for Academic Freedom Safe Havens: Outline of a Research Agenda. Journal of Higher Education in Africa/Revue De L'enseignement Supérieur En Afrique, 16(1-2), 1–24. https://www.codesria.org/spip.php?article2983&lang=en

Zeleza, P. T. (1997). Academic Freedom in the North and South: An African Perspective. Academe, 83(6), 16–21. https://doi.org/10.2307/40251188

Zeleza, P. T. (2006, August 30). Beyond Afropessimism: Historical accounting of African universities. *Pambazuka News,* 263. https://www.pambazuka.org/governance/beyond-afropessimism-historical-accounting-african-universities

Zoubir, Y. H. (2015). Algeria's Roles in the OAU/African Union: From National Liberation Promoter to Leader in the Global War on Terrorism. Mediterranean Politics, 20(1), 55–75. https://doi.org/10.1080/13629395.2014.921470

Zoubir, Y. H. (2019). The Politics of Algeria: Domestic Issues and International Relations. Taylor & Francis. https://books.google.de/books?id=j6S-DwAAQBAJ https://doi.org/10.4324/978042944749